HOW N(

CRASH

REG LOCAL

Follow me on Twitter

@RegLocal

& Look out for my Youtube Channel

ISBN-13: 978-1530991402
ISBN-10: 1530991404

For Jane.

And for all the others.

Also by Reg Local

Advanced & Performance Driving

CONTENTS

Introduction (Jane's Story)   **8**

Notes on the Statistics   **16**

1   **Driver/Rider Error or Reaction**   **22**
Driver/Rider Failed to Look Properly   22
Driver/Rider failed to judge other person's path or speed   32
Poor turn or manoeuvre   38
Loss of control   39
Sudden braking   49
Swerved   50
Junction Overshoot   51
Too close to cyclist, horse rider or pedestrian   54
Failed to signal or misleading signal   57
Junction restart (moving off at junction)   59

2   **Behaviour or inexperience**   **62**
Driver/Rider careless, reckless or in a hurry   62
Learner or inexperienced driver/rider   65
Aggressive driving   67
Driver/Rider nervous, uncertain or panic   76
Unfamiliar with model of vehicle   77
Inexperience of driving on the left   81
Driving too slow for conditions or slow vehicle (e.g. tractor)   82

3   **Injudicious action**   **84**
Travelling Too Fast for Conditions   85

Following too close   89
Exceeding speed limit   97
Disobeyed Give Way or Stop sign or markings   101
Disobeyed automatic traffic signal   108
Cyclist entering road from pavement   112
Illegal turn or direction of travel   114
Disobeyed pedestrian crossing facility   115
Vehicle Travelling Along Pavement   121
Disobeyed Double White Lines   122

4   **Road environment contributed**   **126**
Slippery road (due to weather)   126
Road layout (e.g. bend, hill, narrow road)   132
Deposit on road (e.g. oil, mud, chippings)   133
Animal or object in carriageway   135
Poor or defective road surface   137
Slippery inspection cover or road marking   137
Inadequate or masked signs or road markings   138
Temporary road layout (e.g. contraflow)   139
Defective traffic signals   140
Traffic calming (e.g. road humps, chicane)   140

5   **Impairment or distraction**   **142**
Driver/Rider impaired by alcohol   142
Driver/Rider impaired by drugs (illicit or
medicinal)   161
Recreational Drugs   162
Prescription Drugs   199
Distraction in vehicle   201
Driver/Rider illness or disability, mental or
physical   208
Fatigue   213
Distraction outside vehicle   216
Rider wearing dark clothing   218
Not displaying lights at night or in poor visibility   218
Driver using mobile phone   224

Uncorrected, defective eyesight   229

6   **Pedestrian only (casualty or uninjured)**   **232**

7   **Vision affected by external factors**   **240**
Stationary or parked vehicle(s)   240
Dazzling sun   247
Rain, sleet, snow, or fog   248
Vehicle blind spot   253
Road layout (e.g. bend, winding road, hill crest)   258
Vegetation   258
Buildings, road signs, street furniture   258
Dazzling headlights   259
Spray from other vehicles   261
Visor or windscreen dirty, scratched or frosted etc.   262

8   **Special Codes**   **264**
Other   264
Emergency vehicle on a call   265
Vehicle door opened or closed negligently   268
Stolen vehicle   269
Vehicle in course of crime   269

9   **Vehicle defects**   **272**
Defective brakes   272
Tyres illegal, defective or under inflated   276
Defective steering or suspension   280
Overloaded or poorly loaded vehicle or trailer   282
Defective lights or indicators   282
Defective or missing mirrors   282

10   **Are Driving Standards in the UK Getting Worse?**   **285**

Introduction

Jane's Story

Sunday 31st July 1994

Jane had just turned 20 a couple of weeks ago. She was an outgoing, fun-loving girl who had just come back from her first holiday abroad with her boyfriend, Alan. Jane had an unremarkable but happy childhood, brought up with an older brother and working-class parents in a semi-detached house next to a busy main road on the outskirts of town.

Jane had left school at 16 and decided to work rather than go to college. She got a job with the county council, running the mobile libraries. It was a fairly ordinary admin job, but she enjoyed it and she made lots of friends in the office. She didn't earn much, but when she reached 17, she could afford driving lessons and passed her test the first time round. She saved up some more and then bought her first car - a Vauxhall Nova saloon in red. She ran around in the Nova for a year or so, and then swapped it for a Mk 2 Fiesta.

She was a safe, careful and considerate driver. Much more so than her brother, who was a bit of a speed-freak. Jane's parents worried whenever her brother went out in his car, but they'd both sat next to Jane and seen what a careful driver she was, so they worried much less when Jane was out in her car.

On that particular evening, Jane had visited Alan at his parent's house a couple of miles away. Alan didn't drive, and so he relied on Jane doing most of the running about. She had work the next day and she was looking forward to going in and showing off her tan, so at about 10.30 that night, she set off to drive home where her parents were in, watching television.

Her route took her along a couple of minor roads and then onto the main road which ran out of town, towards her home.

Meanwhile, a young man had been into town to meet up with some of his friends. He was in his early 20s and liked his cars. He had a job at a local garden centre, with which he funded his car - a Vauxhall Cavalier SRi. It cost him quite a lot to insure and run, but it was worth it, because he enjoyed driving it, and above everything else, he enjoyed driving it *fast*.

He had a few drinks with some friends at a pub which was popular with local youngsters. He didn't think that he was affected by the alcohol at all and felt fine to drive home. His route home was similar to the route that Jane was taking at the same time.

On the way out of town, the young man in the Cavalier was overtaken at speed by another young man in a red BMW, with a private plate. "Flashy sod" thought the Cavalier driver, and decided to show the BMW driver the error of his ways.

Both drivers were of a similar mind-set. The Cavalier driver wanted to overtake the BMW to show him who was best. The BMW driver wanted to keep the Cavalier behind him to show him who was best. They ended up in a race.

Meanwhile, Jane was still on her way home.

The BMW and Cavalier continued racing along the main road out of town. The speed limit is 40mph on that road, because it's lined with residential properties and minor junctions. These days, its width is restricted with cycle lanes and central bollards, and there are now a number of speed cameras along the road. In 1994, however, it was just a wide A-road on which 40mph could sometimes seem a little slow.

Very slow in fact, compared with the 85-90mph that the BMW and Cavalier were now travelling at, with barely a cars length between the two vehicles.

Jane was getting close to home now in her Fiesta. Her parent's house was on the right and so she checked her mirrors, indicated right, moved towards the centre-line and then started to slow down in preparation for turning into the driveway. It was quite busy for that time of night and because of the amount of on-coming traffic, Jane had to stop and wait next to the centre-line until a suitable gap appeared.

A couple of hundred yards behind, the BMW and the Cavalier were still racing each other at 85 - 90mph. They overtook several cars, still with no more than 1-2 car lengths between them. The next car they needed to pass was a Mazda MX-5.

The BMW driver saw the situation ahead, and worked out that he could *just* get past the Mazda with enough time to allow him to swerve left and get up the inside of Jane's Fiesta.

The Cavalier driver, on the other hand, did not have the same view as the BMW driver. He was blindly following the BMW into every overtake, assuming that, because it was safe for the BMW, it was also safe for him.

He had not seen Jane's Fiesta.

The BMW passed the Mazda, did a quick flick left and missed Jane's car by inches. The Cavalier driver, however, did not.

He did manage to brake, but only for a very short distance before the impact, and in those pre-ABS days, his locked wheels didn't slow him by much. He hit the rear of Jane's car whilst still travelling at between 56 and 64mph. The impact pushed Jane's car into the path of the oncoming traffic and she was then hit head-on by a car which was travelling towards her at around 40mph. That car was then struck by the car behind, which gave Jane's car a third impact.

It was a few minutes before the emergency services were contacted, as this was in the days before mobile phones had become commonplace.

I was a young police officer in 1994 – I was stationed nearby and although I was just an ordinary patrol officer at the time, I attended the scene of the accident.

The specialist police traffic officers arrived a couple of minutes before me, but this wasn't long enough for them to establish who was involved and to stop me before I arrived at the scene.

Jane was my sister.

She was still alive when I arrived - the fire brigade cut the roof off her car and a couple of emergency doctors were tending to her. She was in the best possible hands. It took them nearly an hour to get her out of the car, but she was being cared for as well as if she'd been on a hospital ward.

Our parents were inside the house, unable to go and look at what was happening. I had to act as a go-between, reassuring them that she was alive and that things might be ok, but knowing deep down, having been to quite a few bumps, that this was very serious, and likely to get worse.

The ambulance set off with Jane at about midnight, with both doctors still working on her. My parents and I were taken to the hospital by one of the traffic officers - a friend of mine.

On arrival at the hospital, one of the emergency doctors gave us the worst possible news. Jane had died just as the ambulance had arrived at the hospital. Her injuries were very severe and there was nothing they could do to save her.

The Cavalier driver survived, albeit with some very serious injuries. He was convicted of causing death by dangerous driving and sentenced to 3 years in prison, with a 5-year ban. Two other innocent drivers received serious and life-changing injuries in the accident.

Despite extensive police enquiries, the BMW driver was never identified.

But he knows who he is.

I always viewed fatal accidents as something which happened to someone else - something interesting to deal with at work, and something tragic to read about in the paper, just before I turned the page to see what's on telly tonight.

Until it happened to us.

To say that losing someone in a road accident is a profoundly life-changing experience would be a major understatement. No-one should have to bury their children, and no-one should have to go through what my parents went through.

There are still approximately 1500 families who go through a similar experience every year in the UK.

That's 29 families a week – 4 or 5 families *every day* who experience the pain, grief and devastation of losing someone they love in a road accident.

You might think that, if you consider just how many vehicles use our roads every day, it's inevitable that people will sometimes die as a result of travelling on the roads. This is true, to a certain extent, but let's not get caught up too much in the statistics for now.

This book is actually about *you*. It's about what *you* can do to avoid being involved in an accident. Not just the very worst serious and fatal accidents, but *any* accident at all, because even the most minor damage-only accident is an embuggerance of paperwork, cost, insurance companies, cost, more paperwork and more cost.

I've examined the most common causes of road accidents and written some very straightforward advice on how to avoid making the mistakes which lead to road accidents.

I'm not on a road safety crusade, I'm not a road safety campaigner and I'm definitely not anti-car/bike/vehicle. Quite the opposite, in fact – I have always been a huge motoring enthusiast and to this day I love cars and driving.

I'm also not here to press home the well-worn and boring road safety messages we're all aware of – the dogmatic "speed kills", "don't drink and drive", "don't text and drive" messages we hear on an almost daily basis. In fact, when you get to those sections of the book, you might be amazed by how *few* accidents are actually caused by speeding, drink driving and texting at the wheel.

That's not to say that these activities aren't risky – they certainly are, but the vast majority of accidents are actually caused by people simply not paying attention – *far* more accidents, in fact, than *all* of those caused by people speeding, drink driving and texting combined.

It's not an advanced driving book either (I've already written one of those if you're interested! *) – it's a book for anyone with any level of driving experience, from learners through to experienced advanced drivers. There are no huge changes you need to make to how you drive your car – just some simple, straightforward advice on how to look and how to think about driving.

If just one person reads this book, and avoids an accident as a result, I'll feel as though the effort I've put into writing it has been worthwhile.

Let me know if it's you!

* *"Advanced & Performance Driving" by Reg Local*

NOTES ON THE STATISTICS

Road accidents are very complicated events. There is rarely (if ever) one *single* cause of a road accident. Even the most straightforward rear-end shunt type accident may be caused by a combination of several different things. The driver behind may have been distracted (1), using their mobile phone (2), driving a car with defective brakes (3) and driving too close (4), whilst the driver in front may have braked suddenly to avoid a cat in the road (5).

So a simple two-vehicle shunt could be caused by a combination of at least 5 or 6 separate causes, which, when combined in just the right order at just the right time, end up with one car crashing into the rear of another – followed by the inevitable swearing, inconvenience, more swearing, cost, more inconvenience and some additional swearing...

These individual causes are referred to as **"contributory factors"**. They are factors which have contributed towards causing the accident. Get used to that term – you'll see it a lot throughout this book.

When the police attend a road accident, once the casualties have been carted off to the hospital, the wrecked vehicles have been moved, and the road has been cleared, the attending police officer is required to fill out an accident report.

If you're ever in any doubt about the amount of paperwork that police officers have to deal with on a daily basis, have a look at a police road traffic accident report. It's an A4 sized booklet of around 11 or 12 pages, onto which the officer must write all manner of information about the accident – who was involved, their injuries, the vehicles involved, the road and junction type, a description of the damage, directions of travel etc. etc.

Some of the information on the form is useful to the reporting officer and helps them in determining the cause(s) of the accident and whether any formal action, prosecutions etc. should follow.

A significant part of the accident form, however, is primarily for statistical purposes. The officer is asked to make a choice of up to six contributory factors, from a list of 78. These 78 contributory factors cover 99% of all occurrences which lead to road accidents. They are organised into 9 sub-headings:

1. **Driver error or reaction**
2. **Behaviour or inexperience**
3. **Injudicious action**
4. **Road environment contributed**
5. **Impairment or distraction**
6. **Pedestrian only**
7. **Vision affected by external factors**
8. **Special codes**
9. **Vehicle defects**

The officer will choose the factors which they think contributed *most* to the accident and will list them in order of how much they think the factors contributed to the accident.

These statistics are then recorded locally by the police accident clerk, and then submitted to the Department for Transport (DFT), who collate all the statistics and publish them annually. The statistics are published every September for the *previous* year, so at the time this book was first published (May 2016), the most recent available figures were for the year January to December 2014.

The statistics are accessible via the DFT's website and are used in a variety of ways by many different organisations and individuals.

And here's where I come in. I've analysed the statistics and looked in detail at every one of the 78 contributory factors. I've looked at how these contributory factors arise, and how you can avoid making those mistakes. In addition, I've also examined how you can look for, and identify those other road users who make these mistakes, and I've suggested some strategies and tips on how to avoid being involved in *someone else's* accident.

I've published each chapter in order of precedence, so the first chapter – the contributory factors under the heading of "Driver error or reaction" – are a factor in 72% of all accidents.

At the start of each chapter I've included the percentage of accidents caused by each sub-heading and I've also done the same for every contributory factor.

The less mathematically challenged amongst you will probably notice that if you add up all the percentages for each contributory factor, it totals far more than 100% (I think they add up to 176). This is because the attending police officer can choose up to six contributory factors from the list, so one accident will include several contributory factors.

The other thing to bear in mind is that these accident statistics relate to *reportable accidents only*. The police only submit reports in relation to accidents which have led to at least one person being injured. There are three levels of injury – **minor** (such as bruising, soreness and soft tissue damage), **serious** (anything from a broken arm or leg, up to very serious, life-changing spinal or head injuries) and **fatal** (where one or more people die as a result of the injuries they receive in the accident). Fatal accidents do not include people who die behind the wheel and then *subsequently* crash.

So the statistics I refer to in this book relate only to accidents in which at least one person has received some form of injury. They do not relate to the many thousands of non-injury accidents which occur every month in the UK. In my experience, however, the contributory factors – and the statistics relating to injury accidents – are mirrored almost exactly by those of non-injury accidents.

In other words – accidents happen for the same reasons, irrespective of whether someone is hurt or not.

To give you some perspective on the numbers of accidents which occur in the UK, here's the raw figures:

There were a total of 115,673 road accidents reported in the UK in 2014. That's 2,224 accidents per week or 317 accidents per day.

Of those, 96,033 were classed as minor injury accidents – 1,847 per week or 263 per day.

18,097 were classed as serious injury accidents – that's 348 people every week – almost 50 people every day who receive serious, live-changing injuries.

And in 2014, 1,543 fatal accidents occurred. Nearly 30 people every week – more than 4 people died *every day* in road accidents in the UK.

Now, these figures are actually much better than they used to be even 10 years ago, particularly when you take into account the number of vehicles on the road (in the region of 35,000,000 in 2014) and the amount of miles travelled by road every day in the UK.

It's still pretty horrific though, to think that over 4 people are being killed and almost 50 seriously injured *every day* just travelling around, going about their daily business.

Makes you think, doesn't it?

So, let's crack on and have a look at **How Not to Crash.**

1. Driver/Rider Error or Reaction (72% of All Accidents)

Driver/Rider Failed to Look Properly   44%

44% of all road accidents are caused by drivers not looking properly.

How can this be possible? How can almost half of drivers who crash not be looking properly? Looking is surely the one thing we should all be doing all the time when we're driving?

You'd like to think so, wouldn't you? But of course, life is never that simple, so here are my tips for avoiding being involved in an accident due to someone simply not looking properly.

Firstly, CONCENTRATE. Can you remember how much you had to concentrate when you first started driving? The simple actions involved in pressing the brake, turning the steering wheel and moving the gear-lever took up pretty much all of your mental capacity. In fact, whilst you were concentrating on operating the controls, your instructor was watching the traffic and looking out for hazards on the road on your behalf.

But, with practice and experience, you probably found that you had to think less and less about controlling the car – setting off, changing gear and steering became almost second nature and you could almost carry out those simple actions without thinking about them at all. For a learner, this is the point where they can start to really concentrate on what's happening outside the car – where to look, how to approach hazards, how fast (or slow) to drive, what's next...

As drivers develop, pass their test and gain experience, that "second nature" mentality starts to creep into every aspect of their driving. As well as giving less and less thought to operating the car's controls, they give less and less thought to how they approach junctions, vehicles and other hazards.

Driving becomes "routine" – something we do without giving it too much thought, much like many other things that we've done a thousand times before. Making a cup of tea, having a shower, vacuuming the carpet, sending a text – these are all actions that at one time or another we've had to learn and concentrate on, but over time we've become able to do them almost automatically without thinking.

Have you ever driven to work, or to the supermarket, or to somewhere else you drive to regularly and had absolutely no recollection of the journey? Did you drive through a red light?

Did you cut someone up in traffic? Can you remember if you locked your car? It's very common to forget the details of journeys if you're not concentrating on your driving.

The reason you can't remember your journey is that you're thinking about other things – what have you got on at work today? What shopping do you need? What shall we have for tea? You're thinking about other things all the time, because driving doesn't really take up much of your mental capacity

The difference between making tea or having a shower and driving a car is that showering and tea making don't involve moving a ton and a half of metal at speed along a road populated by idiots in other lumps of metal also travelling at speed with cyclists, child pedestrians, animals and tractors thrown into the mix.

There are far more risks involved in driving than almost all our other daily tasks combined, but because we generally arrive at our destinations unscathed and undamaged, we don't consider those risks and we habitually lose concentration when driving.

So how do you improve your concentration?

Firstly, remember what you're doing. Don't let your mind wander too far from the fact that you're driving a car at speed in a potentially very dangerous environment. I know you might have had a bad day at work, your partner is mad with you, the kids are screaming on the back seat, you're worried about an unexpected bill, you're wondering what to wear tonight and your dog's been taken ill, but it's important to set these things aside when you get into the driver's seat.

Try this – if you've got a thousand things going on in your head, instead of getting in to the car, putting your seatbelt on, sticking the key in the ignition and going for first gear, try just getting into the car, shutting the door and sitting there for a few seconds – no more than 5 or 10 seconds is enough. Take that time to gather your thoughts, set your other issues aside and remind yourself you're about to drive a car and it'll need your full attention.

Be curious and use your imagination. Look at every junction or hazard and imagine what might go wrong. Could a car pull out on you? Might a child run out from behind those parked cars? Could that wobbly cyclist fall off in front of you? If you start to imagine what might happen, your predictions will sometimes come true! The car will pull out, the child will run out and the wobbly cyclist will fall off. Instead of being surprised by these things going wrong, if you've imagined them happening, you'll be prepared and you'll be much less likely to have an accident.

Tied in with using your imagination is the skill of making driving plans. Once you've started imagining what might happen, you can build on this skill by planning what you should do *if* those things happen. So, if that car *does* pull out in front of you, you'll brake and steer round it. If a child *does* run out from behind the parked cars, you'll brake and avoid them. If the wobbly cyclist *does* fall off, you'll avoid hitting them (once you've stopped laughing, of course).

Using your imagination and making driving plans will hugely improve your ability to maintain a good level of concentration even on your most mundane, everyday journeys.

On longer journeys, it's easy to let your concentration slip, particularly if you're travelling for several hours on motorways, which can be quite monotonous. Take regular breaks, keep hydrated, make sure you eat regularly so that your blood sugar doesn't drop too low and have a rest, preferably away from the car, if you start feeling tired.

There are other bars to concentration, such as mobile phones and alcohol/drugs, but I'll cover these in a later chapter.

How do you look?

No, I don't mean how does your hair look? Or do those shoes go with that skirt? Or does your bum look big?

I mean, how do you look down the road and around you when you're driving? It sounds like a pretty stupid question to start with (I look down the road – what else is there to say?), but there's actually a lot more to it than you might think.

Firstly, you need to understand that your eyes work in a specific way – and it's not a way which is always well suited to driving a car or riding a motorbike. As you read this book, you're looking straight ahead at the pages, and you also have a wide field of view of everything else around you – you may be looking at the book or e-reader, but you can also see the rest of the room, or the other people on the train, or the beach and the sea (lucky sod!) to the left and right, above and below the page you're actually looking at. This is commonly referred to as your peripheral vision.

But peripheral vision isn't really as good as you might think it is. Try this little exercise - keep looking at this page and reading these words, and at the same time, try to pick out some detail of your surrounding area *without taking your eyes off the words.*

Try to pick out what that movement is through the window, or what the passenger next to you is wearing, or how many people are swimming in the sea (lucky sod!). It's not possible to make out that level of detail in your peripheral vision.

You might be able to make out some movement, or some basic colours or shapes, but if you're not looking directly at something, your peripheral vision only really gives a visual "frame" to the detail that you're looking directly at.

Let's move that little exercise on a little and make it more focussed. Keep looking at these words, but try to read the words in the paragraph below, *without taking your eyes off these words.* It's still not possible is it? You can make out words and spaces and paragraphs, but you can't actually read the words, can you?

Now try it with the *line* below. Look at the words on this line, but try to read the line directly below. Now it's just about getting possible to make out letters and words, but it's still not easy to read in this way – let's face it, you need to be looking directly at the words to be able to read them properly. But how small are the words? Compared with your field of vision, they're tiny, so although we feel like we've got a nice, wide field of vision, we can only actually look at detail in a very narrow area right in the centre of our field of vision. Right where we're actually looking at the time, in fact.

Over millions of years, our bodies have developed strategies to deal with this limitation in our vision. Try this little exercise – sit opposite a friend (it's better with a friend, as strangers give you a funny look if you ask them to do it), and ask them to stare at your right eye and then your left eye, and then keep switching between your left and right eye every second or so. Watch their eyes as they look from left to right – they flick, very quickly in an almost insect-like manner.

Then try the same exercise, but this time with yourself in the mirror. You'll look from eye to eye, but you won't notice the flicking motion at all – our brains have evolved to ignore the blur when your eyes are moving, and focus only when your eyes are stationary, in between the "flicks". Even if you try to look smoothly from left to right in a long arc, your eyes are actually flicking and stopping, flicking and stopping constantly, but because your brain ignores the flicking, it'll look to you as though you're just smoothly moving your eyes from left to right in one movement.

So, we can only focus on detail in a very small part of our field of vision, but our eyes compensate by flicking about at high speed and allowing us to focus in detail on lots of things in a short space of time. If you were going to design eyes from scratch for driving, they wouldn't be like that, would they? I can't imagine Google or Tesla or whoever else is developing driverless cars have designed limited field, flicky cameras. I imagine they're developing cameras which constantly monitor everything that's happening 360° around the car at all times. A camera like this won't miss anything, and won't be looking in the wrong direction at the wrong time. It is, for want of a better expression, an *all seeing eye.*

The All Seeing Eye

So, obviously, we're biologically limited and we're not going to evolve 360° HD eyes any time soon, so how do we make the best of what we've got? How do we train ourselves to use our eyes *as though* they are 360° HD cameras? It's not as difficult as you might think.

Firstly, when you're looking along the road, you should try to develop a system for *where* to look. My system is:

Far Distance

Middle Distance

Near Distance

Sides

Rear

So let's go through each of those in turn and see how it works.

Far Distance I start by looking as far ahead as it's possible to see. On some roads, this can be right up to the horizon, and on others your view will be more limited – perhaps a few hundred yards at most. Starting in the far distance allows you to build a mental picture of where the road is going and what hazards you're likely to encounter further down the road.

Middle Distance I hesitate to set an actual distance on this – the middle distance can vary as much as the far distance can, but in practice, it's usually halfway between you and the far distance. Looking into the middle distance allows you to see and plan for hazards which you'll encounter *next*. In other words, you'll be looking at the hazards you'll be dealing with after the one you're currently dealing with.

Near Distance This is the stuff immediately in front of you – the stuff you're actually driving round or through at the present time. The cyclist you're passing, the corner you're driving round, the roundabout you're on or the pedestrian crossing you're stopping at.

Sides Without teaching you to suck eggs *too* much, this is the stuff that's happening either side of you, alongside you, in your "blind" spots, and over your shoulders. If you're keeping good observations, things alongside you shouldn't take you by surprise.

Rear Centre mirror, side mirrors and occasional shoulder checks should allow you to keep a good, clear picture of everything that's going on behind you, but I don't just mean the occasional glance behind – you need to employ a similar technique to when you're looking forwards – a mirror check should start in the far distance, then move to the middle and near distances.

Scanning

When you're practising this "all seeing eye" technique, try to combine it with another technique, referred to as *scanning*. Scanning is a continual visual "sweep", whereby you continually move your eyes around, picking out potentially hazardous situations which might cause you problems as you approach them. Let's use a line of parked cars as an example:

Start by looking in the far distance to see if there are any cars approaching from the opposite direction which you might need to give priority to.

Then look along the line of parked cars to see if any have brake lights on, doors closing/opening, indicators or any other little clues that cars might be moving off or doors opening into your path.

As you pass the parked cars, keep a look out for movements of feet underneath the cars you're passing which might be someone about to cross the road.

Check to the sides for cyclists or other hazards, and check your mirrors for vehicles approaching from behind.

Use the same approach at junctions – don't just take a quick glance left and right – a quick glance will not allow you to take in enough detail. Instead, use the all seeing eye approach, take a second longer to look far, mid and near distance. A slightly longer scan will allow you to better assess the speed of approaching vehicles and you'll be far less likely to miss more vulnerable road users such as cyclists or motorcyclists.

Your eyes should never be still when you're driving – if you stare at something for too long, you'll exclude all the other hazards from your driving plans and you're far more likely to miss something important and make a mistake which could lead to an accident.

Other Drivers

Improving your own observation skills is all well and good, but what about everyone else? 42% of them aren't looking properly, so even if you're doing everything right, how do you protect yourself from all the other blind idiots out there?

Start by assuming that no-one has seen you. If you keep at the back of your mind the possibility that any of the other road users out there may pull out on you. Swerve into your lane or step out in front of you, then you'll always have a plan in mind to help you avoid an accident.

When you see another vehicle waiting in a junction, check to see whether the driver has looked in your direction. At the same time, keep an eye out for whether their wheels are stationary or moving, and whether their brake lights (if they're visible) are on or off, or – even worse – have just gone off.

If you spot a car waiting in a junction and the driver isn't looking in your direction, the brake lights go off and the wheels start to turn, there's a better-than-good chance that they're about to pull out in front of you, so lift off the accelerator, move towards the centre line and be ready to brake.

And consider sounding your horn.

Horn use isn't always appropriate – if you blast your horn after someone has already pulled out, for instance, there's a chance they may panic and stop right in your path and make a bad situation worse.

If, however, you're picking up clues that a car *might* pull into your path because the driver hasn't seen you, then a horn warning can be a good idea. Give a short blast on the horn and look for a reaction from the driver. They may hit the brakes, look in your direction or flick you a middle finger. It doesn't really matter – all that matters is that they have seen you and you've prevented them from pulling out by getting their attention.

Horns are extremely misused these days, but this is an example of how to use one correctly.

So there you go – concentrate, learn how to look and assume no-one has seen you. Easy!

Don't be one of the 44%!

Driver failed to judge other person's path or speed 22%

Have you ever spoken to someone who had an accident and heard them say something like: "the car came out of nowhere"? Maybe you've had an accident or near miss yourself and felt like another vehicle had appeared from nowhere – you pulled up at the junction, looked, didn't see anything, pulled out and...

"The car/bike/motorbike just seemed to appear from nowhere."

Of course, the vehicle didn't come from nowhere – there isn't a fleet of magically appearing ghost cars and bikes out there randomly appearing and causing accidents. It's just that other road users – for one reason or another – simply don't see them.

Whenever you drive a car, you're constantly judging the paths and speeds of other road users. You don't even realise you're doing it most of the time – it's another one of those skills which we carry out so regularly that it becomes almost second-nature and with experience, we develop the ability to judge paths and speeds without consciously thinking about it.

And there's the problem.

Making a judgement on the direction and speed of other road users is an absolutely crucial skill, yet most of the time, most drivers aren't giving it any conscious thought – they're just letting their peripheral vision and their unconscious mind sort it out for them.

Now, you don't really have to actively think about picking up the television controller and changing channels do you? You might actively think about changing over from Homes Under the Hammer to watch Loose Women, but the actions involved – reaching for the controller, picking it up, finding the channel button, pressing it and putting it down again – don't actually require you to actively think about what you're doing. You just do it.

And that's fine – if you get any of those actions wrong, the worst that can happen is that you press the wrong button and end up watching Strictly Come Big Brother Bake-Off or some other such tripe for a couple of seconds before correcting your mistake.

But we're effectively using a very similar mental process when we're driving – and particularly when we're driving on roads we're very familiar with. You approach the same "T" junction every day at the same time, you have a quick look right as you approach the junction, it looks clear, you take first gear and turn left. All pretty much done without giving any conscious thought to the process.

But think about that for a minute – you're trusting your unconscious mind and your peripheral vision to make a clear judgement on whether there are any vehicles approaching from the right, and how fast they are travelling towards you – cyclists, motorcyclists, buses, trucks carrying sulphuric acid or high explosives…

You get my drift.

And most of the time, this reliance on your subconscious goes unpunished. Most of the time, your unconscious brain gets it right, and you continue along your journey, undamaged, unbruised and unburned to death in a horrific fireball & explosion.

But 22% of accidents are caused by people failing to judge another road users path or speed – in more than a fifth of all accidents, our unconscious mind lets us down badly and we make a poor judgement which leads to an accident. That doesn't include the millions of near-misses and near-disasters we have every year – just the accidents.

So how can you improve?

Try Colouring in!

You've all done some colouring in haven't you? You know – colouring books, with black-and-white line drawings and some coloured felt-tipped pens to colour the picture with?

I know it may be some time since you've actually done some colouring in, but I want you to think about the process of colouring in and apply it to how you look down the road. Let's use a straightforward "T" junction as an example.

When you pull up to a "T" junction and you look right and left, imagine that you first see a black and white line drawing of the road. In other words, you can see the basic shape and image of the road, but it's lacking detail and doesn't give you enough information to help you decide if it's safe to pull out or not.

This is where you need to do some colouring in – with your eyes. You need to quickly move your eyes over the whole picture, colouring in the detail. Start with a glance at the road layout – does it give you a good, clear view or is your vision obscured? Have a look at any approaching vehicles – make a very quick mental note of their positions. Look for other junctions to the left and right of the road – are there any vehicles likely to emerge? What other hazards are there? Pedestrians? Cyclists? Motorcyclists in particular are extremely vulnerable and can easily be hidden by road furniture or even your car's windscreen pillar.

This process may sound like it'll take ages, but it really doesn't need to – it can be done in a very short time once you've trained your eyes to move around the picture, colouring in the detail (less than a second at a well-sighted junction – perhaps a bit longer at a busy or less well-sighted junction).

This next bit is very important – once you've quickly coloured your picture in, you should mentally "save" the image before moving on to the next step.

The Principle of the Second look

At our imaginary "T" junction, you'll start with a look to the right (in the UK, the closest and most hazardous vehicles will be approaching from the right – if you're reading this in a cack-handed country where they drive on the wrong side, you should start with a look to the left).

Quickly colour that picture in, then look to the left and do the same. Then look right again – you should never base a decision to "go" on a single glance in each direction. You need to use *the principle of the second look* to compare your second look with your mentally "saved" first picture. That comparison will allow you to consider how much the approaching road users have moved between your first and second look.

If they haven't moved much, they're travelling quite slowly. If they have moved a lot, then they're likely to be travelling at a higher speed.

This may sound like fairly obvious stuff, but remember, over a fifth of all motorists get this wrong on a regular basis and end up injuring or killing themselves or someone else.

Keep that in mind the next time you're approaching a junction & apply my basic principles:

Colour the picture in;

Save the image;

Take a second look;

Compare the two pictures.

A Couple of Other Tips

Don't trust other people's signals

It's quite common for other drivers or riders to accidentally leave an indicator on when, in fact, they've no intention of turning off. If you're waiting at a junction and you see a vehicle approaching with an indicator on, look for another sign that they're going to turn off – slowing down, for example, or moving their position – just something to confirm that they're intending to do what the signal is suggesting.

Waiting a second or two for this confirmation could save you from a bump.

Never make assumptions

It's very easy – particularly on roads you're very familiar with, to start making assumptions. You've driven along a road many hundreds of times, and no-one has ever pulled out in front of you. There's never been a cyclist, or a horse, around that blind corner and a child has never run out from behind a parked car.

So because these things have never happened, they're never *going* to happen, are they?

Are they?

Of course they are – one day. And it might be today.

So try to drive every road as though you've never seen it before – even if it's the road you live on. Look carefully at every junction for vehicles that might emerge, look underneath parked cars for movements of feet, and at every corner, ask yourself if you could stop in the distance you can see to be clear.

Because the one day someone does do something unexpected, daft or inexplicable, you'll deal with it much more effectively if you drive without making assumptions.

Poor turn or manoeuvre   16%

Unfortunately, this accident cause isn't further defined in any way and if I think back to the days when I used to fill in accident reports, it's a sort of "cover-all" factor for when the officer can't really fit the circumstances of an accident into any other of the cause factors.

As Sniff Petrol's Detective Inspector Mark Blundell would say *"What done happen here was, to be fair, that an IC1 male was done proceeding in a westerly direction when he done make what, in fairness, was a poor turn or manoeuvre and done caused a road traffic accident".*

So (and at the risk of looking like I'm copping out of this one), I think every aspect of making a poor turn or manoeuvre is covered in the other sections of this book. With that in mind, to avoid repeating myself – and to avoid causing concern for my children who might start looking for a care home for me - as they keep threatening to do for telling the same story over and over again – I'll leave this subject alone.

Loss of control   13%

I don't know about you, but I honestly thought this percentage would be much higher. If the subject of road accidents comes up in a conversation, the first thing I imagine is a car skidding and sliding off the road and colliding with something else, but the statistics show that only 13% of accidents involve a "loss of control".

Still, 13% of reportable accidents still equates to well over 15,000 injury or fatal road accidents per year and many more non-injury accidents, so it's well worth us examining the subject in detail and exploring how you can avoid losing control.

Let's start by defining "loss of control".

I would suggest that the definition should be something like *"where a driver makes an input with a cars controls, but the car does not react in the way the driver intended".*

Does that sound sufficiently "Road Traffic Act" to you? It's not – I've just made it up, but I think it covers the basics – if you turn the wheel and the car doesn't steer as you expected, or press the brakes and it doesn't slow down as expected, or press the accelerator and something else happens – again, unexpectedly – then you've lost control.

Its Skidding really!

If this is all sounding a bit complicated, I'm actually talking about skidding, but some people (some of them experts, and some of them not so much) take pleasure in deliberately skidding cars around, so let's be very clear here – I'm going to tell you how to deal with unintentional and unexpected skidding – not how to drift, drive a rally car or do handbrake turns on McDonalds car park.

If you want to read about that stuff, other "expert" books are available (some with a similar title to this one!).

So - skidding. What is a skid?

In very simple terms, a skid occurs when a cars tyres lose grip with the road surface. There are some technical people who will tell you that a tyre is always skidding slightly, but you should ignore them. I think, for the purposes of this book, we all understand that a tyre usually grips the road surface and when it doesn't, the car will skid.

Three types of skid

There are three main things that you can do as a driver which can lead to a skid – Braking, Steering and Accelerating and I'll look at each in turn, but before I do, you should understand that there is a wealth of information available in books and online which will tell you how to control a skid. You'll find stuff which talks about cadence braking, controlling a slide, counter-steering, opposite lock, and a wealth of other information.

In this book however, I'm going to make it as simple as possible, so to start with, I'm going to assume you drive a modern car – something made in the last 10 years or so – and that it's fitted with a couple of safety features which are pretty much standard on all mass-produced cars these days. Anti-lock brakes (ABS) and Stability Control (ESC or ASC or DSC or any number of other acronyms).

If you're unsure whether your car has these systems fitted, have a look in the owner's manual, or look it up online. You could also check with the manufacturer or dealer, but beware of dealers – every time I go to one I get suckered into buying a new car, so try Google – it's cheaper!

If you drive an older car or a specialised car without these systems fitted, then the following advice on skid control is NOT for you! If you do drive one of these cars, try to get hold of a copy of my book "Advanced & Performance Driving", which includes a whole chapter on the more traditional skid control techniques.

So, let's start by taking a look at the three main causes of skids:

Braking

Skidding under braking used to be very common – if you press the brakes on an older car hard enough, the wheels will "lock up" and stop turning and your car will slide along with its wheels locked solid until the friction with the road surface brings it to a stop – usually in a big cloud of grey tyre smoke accompanied by a loud screeching sound.

The problem with this is that as soon as the wheels stop rotating, the car will just travel in a straight line, so the driver can turn the steering wheel as much as they like and it'll have no effect whatsoever – the car will continue ploughing on in whatever direction it was pointing when the driver started braking.

Now, drivers only usually hit the brakes like this in an emergency, so the car will generally be pointing towards the emergency situation – the child who has run into the road, the cyclist who's fallen off, the overturned petrol tanker – when the brakes then lock up. So skidding under braking can mean you end up having a really bad day.

Anti-Lock Brakes

Car manufacturers have a vested interest in keeping you alive. If you die in an accident, you won't be able to buy another car from them, and if you kill someone else, you may end up in prison or disqualified from driving and unable to buy another car from them. The person you've killed won't be able to buy a car from them either.

So, because they're nice people and they want to carry on selling you cars, they invented anti-lock brakes (usually referred to as ABS). The principle is quite simple – if the car detects that the wheels are locking up, it releases the brakes for a fraction of a second, before re-applying the brakes. It then repeats this cycle – releasing and re-applying the brakes as much as 15 times per second.

The outcome of this very fast on-off-on-off-on-off of the brakes is that the car will stop as quickly and efficiently as possible *without* locking the wheels.

And because the wheels don't lock, the driver can still steer the car – around the child, fallen cyclist or overturned petrol tanker – and avoid the inevitable death, prison, driving ban and associated paperwork.

How do you use anti-lock brakes?

Firstly, you don't actually need to do anything to use your cars ABS system – it's always on, and it's always sitting there ready to step in and help you. Under normal braking, ABS doesn't do anything – the brakes just operate as normal and slow you down nicely without any ABS intervention.

In an emergency, however, the advice is simple...

Brake as hard and as fast as you possibly can and keep the brakes applied hard until you stop!

Seriously – in an emergency, stand on that brake pedal as quickly and as hard as you possibly can, and don't let go till you've stopped. Heave on the brake pedal as though there's a deadly tarantula under your right foot, and try to push the brake pedal out though the cars floor. If you're not lifting yourself up out of your seat, then you're not braking hard enough!

You won't break the pedal – it's stronger than you are – and if you want to stop in the shortest amount of time, then you need to forget about smoothness and finesse, and you need to muller the brake pedal with all your strength!

If you follow this very simple advice, the ABS will activate and the car will brake to a stop in the shortest possible time. You'll feel a vibration – sometimes quite a harsh vibration – through the brake pedal. This is the ABS doing its job and applying the brakes on and off very quickly. Don't worry about the vibration, just keep that pedal mashed into the floor. And here's the second piece of advice relating to ABS...

Don't forget to Steer!

Don't just stare at the approaching accident like a startled rabbit! Steer round it! One of the biggest benefits of ABS is that it allows you to retain some tyre grip for steering whilst braking very hard, so use it! If there's a gap to the left or the right, steer towards it. If there's a choice between hitting a pedestrian or hitting a hedge, steer towards the hedge. Cat or oncoming car? Well, we're into moral dilemmas here, but – and I'm sorry if you're an animal lover – I'd always choose to hit an animal rather than something containing humans. But I'll leave that one up to you.

So there you go – if your car starts to skid under braking, there are two simple things you can do to avoid an accident:

Brake very hard and steer.

Steering

The second cause of skidding I'll discuss is steering.

If you're particularly harsh or rough with a cars steering, or if you drive around a corner too fast, there is a real risk that you'll use up all the available tyre grip and your car will start to skid. This possibility is even greater if you're driving on a particularly slippery road surface.

There are three main types of skid which could occur in these circumstances:

Understeer – the car will steer less than the driver wants it to. It will feel like the car is "pushing on" in a corner and you'll feel like you want to steer more and more in the direction you want to go.

Oversteer – The car will steer *more* than the driver wants it to. The rear of the car will "step out" and the car will feel like it's spinning. You'll feel like you want to steer less, or even steer in the opposite direction.

Four-Wheel Skid – Alternatively known as a four-wheel drift. All four wheels will slide sideways towards the outside of the corner – the car will feel like it's moving sideways and you'll feel like you need to steer more to get the car moving in the right direction.

Cars have a natural tendency towards different kinds of skids, and the main factor which decides a car's tendency is *which wheels are driven.*

There are three main types of drive:

Front-wheel drive – These cars have the engine driving the front wheels and generally have a natural tendency to *understeer.*

Rear-wheel drive – These cars have the engine driving the rear wheels and generally have a natural tendency to *oversteer.*

Four-wheel drive – These cars have the engine driving all four wheels and generally (but not always!) have a tendency to *four-wheel skid.*

Now, this all sounds very beardy-and-flat-cappy and probably doesn't interest those of you who just want to travel from A to B and occasionally to C, so I'm going to make the following advice as simple as possible.

Almost all new cars these days will have some form of stability control fitted. Stability control is a complicated electronic system which constantly monitors how the car is being driven, what direction it's travelling in, how fast all the wheels are turning and a number of other factors. The result of all these measurements is that your car can recognise when it's starting to skid, and it can help you to keep control.

It helps you keep control by adjusting or cutting the throttle (accelerator) and by applying the brakes to individual wheels to help get it pointing back in the direction you intend to go.

So, if, for instance, you are driving too fast around a right-hand bend and your car starts to oversteer (the rear starts to slide out to the left), your car will recognise the skid, cut the throttle and apply the brakes to the rear right-hand wheel only. These actions will help you to keep control and should result in the skid ending very quickly – often before you've even realised it's actually started.

How do you use stability control?

This is the million-dollar question, and the answer is...

Leave it switched on!

That's it really – the system is automatically on whenever you get into your car and switch on the ignition, and unless you switch it off, it'll stay on, quietly keeping an eye on you throughout your journey, ready to intervene if it ever detects the onset of a skid.

These systems can be switched off, but I really don't advise it. Whilst I was researching this book, I corresponded with an engineer who spends his life developing and calibrating these types of safety systems. Here's what he wrote in the subject:

"For the record, despite having spent many years going sideways on ice, test tracks, in muddy forests and yes, even around the occasionally deserted roundabout, the DSC stays firmly ON in my car!"

So if the absolute expert on this subject always leaves his stability control switched on, there is no need whatsoever for you to ever switch yours off. If you're ever tempted to switch it off because you find it cuts in too often, then you need to reevaluate your driving rather than switch the systems off.

Understeer with stability control

If you feel the front of the car sliding a bit wide on a corner or roundabout, just keep steering in the direction you want to go (don't be tempted to add *more* steering – just keep the wheel pointing where you want to go) and lift off the throttle a little. The stability control should do the rest and help to pull you back in line.

Don't press the clutch either – if you do, you take drive away from the wheels and the car cannot do much to help you, so don't press the clutch.

Oversteer with stability control

If you feel the rear of the car starting to slide, just lift off the throttle by about 50% and steer in the direction you want to go. Many people steer *too much* in the opposite direction and this can lead to a secondary – and more severe – skid. So don't counter steer too much – no more than a quarter-to-a-half turn of the steering wheel.

And again, don't press the clutch. The car will do its thing and should help pull you back into line.

What if nothing is working?

If you've tried everything and you're still skidding and it appears that you're going to leave the road, there are two things you should do:

1. Press your brakes as hard as you can and keep them on. This will at least reduce the speed of your car as much as possible before the inevitable impact, and;

2. Look at the gap, and not at the tree. We have a tendency to collide with the things that we're staring at, so don't stare at the tree/lamp post/telegraph pole – stare at the gap between them instead and you should avoid hitting something unpleasant.

Skidding under acceleration

The third cause of skidding is excessive acceleration, which can cause the driven wheels to lose traction with the road and spin unnecessarily quickly. In extreme circumstances, this can cause the car to swerve violently out of control.

Stability control systems also include a system commonly referred to as "traction control". Traction control monitors how fast the driven wheels are turning in comparison with the non-driven wheels, and if it detects one or more wheels spinning, the car will cut the throttle and apply a brake to the spinning wheel(s).

As with my earlier advice, the best thing you can do is leave the system switched on. Like stability control, traction control is "on all the time" and there should never be any reason for you to switch the system off (unless you're stuck in deep snow, which might need a little wheelspin – this is the only circumstance when I would ever turn the system off).

So if you feel the traction control cutting the throttle, your best course of action is to lift off the throttle a little until the wheels have stopped spinning and then reapply the throttle a little more carefully.

Avoid the skid in the first place

If you could train yourself to look for the potential emergencies and slow down early to avoid them; if you could spot the poor road surface or slippery conditions and deal with them sensibly and early; if you could learn to look in the right places and make a driving plan which included all potential emergencies; that'd be better wouldn't it?

Well, you can – that's what advanced driving is all about, so I'd advise you, if it's at all possible, to get some further driver training to improve your observation and anticipation skills. If you can avoid the emergency or the skid in the first place, you're a much better driver than the person who is good at controlling skids, but can't avoid getting into them.

Sudden braking   7%

Sudden braking is included as a contributory factor because it's usually something which catches *other* drivers out. If, for example, you're driving along and an animal runs out in front of you, your normal reaction will probably to be to suddenly brake hard to avoid hitting the animal.

This is fine – for avoiding the animal – but if the driver behind is too close, or not paying attention, then your sudden baking could contribute towards them crashing into the rear of your car.

That may be an extreme example, but many drivers are habitually rough, or harsh with their brakes. I'm sure you've sat alongside a driver who uses the brake pedal like a switch – the brakes are either off or fully on – and every time they stop you're left rocking in your seat and nursing a sore neck & a seatbelt bruise.

These drivers always run the risk of being driven into by inattentive tailgaters and it's worth learning how to brake as smoothly and progressively as possible.

First application of the brakes should be a very light touch - this will start to build up hydraulic pressure in the system and push the brake pads up to the face of the disk. Effectively, you're "taking up the slack" in the system, although the "slack" is actually tiny. Think of the first touch as priming the brakes ready for use.

Then start to apply the brakes very gently. Bear in mind that the first actual pressure that you apply to the pedal will switch on your brake lights, letting following drivers know you're braking and slowing.

Then you should gradually increase the pressure on the brake pedal until you've lost most of the speed you need to lose, before gently easing back off the brake pedal pressure just before you come to a stop – which should be nice and smooth with no jerk when you actually stop.

If you practice every time you drive, you'll avoid the sudden and harsh braking which can often lead to accidents.

You should also look out for the harsh brakers when you're driving and if you spot one, make sure you leave a nice, long gap between your car and there's, so that you don't get caught out.

Swerved   4%

In the same way that harsh braking can cause accidents, harsh steering can also lead to a loss of control. As I mentioned earlier in this chapter, avoiding a skid is much better than correcting one, so if you can learn how to steer smoothly and progressively, you'll be much less likely to end up swerving out of control.

The way to apply steering lock is to turn the wheel slowly at first, build up the speed of the lock application until you're close to having the right amount of lock applied, and then slow down the application again until the wheel is stationary. Starting with a slow, gradual turn of the wheel starts to gently settle the car onto its springs rather than suddenly chucking lock on and expecting the car to go immediately from travelling in a straight line, to turning.

In addition, practice looking further ahead, and planning what you're going to do well in advance of the next hazard. As you get better at planning, you'll find that those occasions when you have to swerve suddenly become less and less frequent.

Junction overshoot   2%

This is an odd one – how do people manage to overshoot junctions? It may be difficult to comprehend, but this one accounts for over 2,500 accidents a year, so let's have a look at how you can avoid these types of accidents.

The primary cause of overshooting is drivers carrying too much speed *right up* to a junction. In other words, they leave their braking too late for the junction and then catch themselves out by overshooting and driving out into the path of other vehicles.

The key to avoiding overshoots is to look well ahead, spot the junction early, work out well in advance where the stop or give way line is and plan your approach with the mind-set that you will have to stop at that line. The term I use (and you'll read about it in more detail elsewhere in the book) is *planning to stop, but looking to go.*

In other words, although you're looking for the opportunity to go at the junction if it's safe, your first – and overriding plan – at a junction must be to stop behind the line.

If you introduce this little phrase to your planning, you'll start to plan your approaches to junctions in a much more structured way and you'll be able to brake early and smoothly, rather than late and heavy, and avoid junction overshoots.

Other Drivers

But what about other drivers? How can you account for the other drivers who don't plan properly and end up overshooting junctions?

The secret – as with many other aspects of driving – is in making driving plans.

As you drive along, you should be constantly looking all around you and then using the information you get from your observations to make driving plans. Those driving plans are based on three things:

1. *What you can see;*

2. *What you can't see, and;*

3. *What you can reasonably expect to happen.*

Number 1 is relatively easy – you see what's up ahead and make your plans based on the things you can see.

Number 2, however, is far more complex and requires an active (but not *over*active) imagination. It requires you to look at the stuff you can see and work out the likely possibilities ahead. It's something which many drivers struggle with at first and is often described in much broader terms like "driver experience" or "time behind the wheel".

I prefer the term "observation links" – when you see something, it may give you a clue, or a "link" to something else which may happen, even though you can't see it yet.

Let me give you an example. You're driving along a road in a residential area and you notice that each house has its dustbins out ready for collection. It's reasonable to assume that the bin men will be somewhere around and so your plan will include the possibility that, round the next corner or junction, you may encounter a bin lorry and bin men in the road.

Here's another. You're driving along on a country road and you pass an entrance to a field. You see fresh muddy tyre tracks leading out of the field and along the road in the direction you're travelling. You make an observation link with the possibility that the tractor that left those marks is probably somewhere up ahead, so your driving plan will now include that possibility.

And a third – this one is far more common and something you should include in your plans at all times. You're driving along a road and you can see that there are several junctions to the left and right up ahead. You cannot see into these junctions, but at any time, a vehicle may pull up to those junctions. Some may pull up correctly, some may overshoot the junctions a little and some may just pull out in front of you without looking.

But for the time being, all you can see are the junctions, so your plan is based on the junctions (that you can see), the vehicles which might be approaching the junctions (that you cannot see), and the fact that some of these vehicles might overshoot or emerge from the junctions carelessly (that you can reasonably expect to happen).

So your driving plan will be to give yourself a zone of relative safety around your car by moving away from the junctions as much as it's safe to do – move a few feet towards the centre-line of the road so that if something does overshoot one of the junctions, you've already moved away from them and any avoiding action you need to take will be kept to a minimum.

One place where you're more likely to encounter overshooting drivers is at motorway junctions with drivers who have just left the motorway. When you've been travelling at higher speeds on the motorway, it can take a short time to readjust to the lower speeds required when you leave the motorway – it's easy to think that you've slowed down to 30mph when, in fact, you're still travelling at 50mph.

If you're leaving a motorway, plan further ahead, and slow your car gradually and progressively on the slip-road well ahead of the junction or roundabout at the end. This is one place where you really shouldn't leave your braking to the last minute.

If you're on normal roads and passing a motorway junction, have a good look at the vehicles approaching the junction or roundabout having left the motorway – are they slowing enough? Will they stop in time? Include these thoughts in your driving plan, move away from the mouth of the junction they're approaching and be ready to stop or avoid the overshooters if they emerge.

Too close to cyclist, horse rider or pedestrian 2%

I've dealt with pedestrians in detail in chapter 6, but it's worth looking at cyclists and horses in detail, as they are very vulnerable road users and there are plenty of things you should, and shouldn't be doing when you pass them on the road.

Let's start with cyclists. If you've ever ridden a bicycle on the road, you'll know how vulnerable you can feel. In a car you're surrounded by a big metal shell, isolated from the elements by a roof and windows, sitting in comfy seats, held in by seatbelts and protected by airbags if things go wrong.

On a bicycle you're surrounded by the outside world, protected from the elements by your clothes and if you're sensible, you're protected by a lightweight helmet if things go wrong. Or by skin and skull if you're not sensible.

I don't cycle these days, but when I was cycling it never ceased to amaze me how close some drivers pass you on the road. It often feels as though they haven't even seen you and being passed with one or two inches to spare is not uncommon.

I don't really understand why people give so little care to passing cyclists – they're only ever one wobble or slip away from falling off right in front of you and your driving plan when approaching cyclists should always include the possibility that they'll fall off in front of you or whilst you're passing them.

The key is to give them enough room. The advice most often dished out is "give them as much room as you would if you were passing a car". But that's nonsense really, isn't it? You're not passing a car – you're passing a cyclist and the risks involved are completely different. So here's my advice when it comes to passing cyclists on the road:

Imagine the cyclist laid on their side – which is where they'll be if they fall off. If you cannot pass a cyclist without leaving enough room for them to fall off without hitting them, you should wait behind them until there is more space. Leave a zone of relative safety equal to the height of the cyclist laid width-ways across the road.

Sometimes there is limited room and if there are oncoming cars preventing you from leaving enough room, then the best advice is to wait behind the cyclist until there *is* enough room. If you do need to pass a cyclist with less room than I describe above, you should do it slowly and not pull back in until you can see the cyclist in your centre rear-view mirror.

Horses

One of my favourite ever letters to Viz comic went like this:

I remember from history lessons seeing drawings of battlefields. There'd be thousands of people with swords, hacking and slashing away, cannons going off left right and centre, and hot tar being poured over castle walls to fend off advancing soldiers. And amongst this carnage would be generals on horseback, marauding through vast swathes of dead and dying with the horses knee deep in mud whilst being attacked with spears. Bloody hell, nowadays if there's a horse rider trotting along a country lane, you have to slow to a crawl so as not to frighten them and give them so wide a birth you need your bloody sat nav to get back to the same bloody road! When did horses become so bloody soft?!

That one still tickles me.

But in reality, horses aren't really soft – I used to regularly see the police mounted branch in action at football matches and in serious public disorder situations, and – believe me – horses can be extremely brave and very intimidating if you're on the wrong side of them, so soft they are definitely not!

They are, however, very easily startled – particularly when they are not mentally prepared for a sudden noise or movement – and in my experience, there are very few things more dangerous than a ton of startled raw horse meat.

So the key thing to consider when passing horses is that you need to do so in such a way that you won't startle the horse – that's it, that's all you have to do – not startle the horse.

The best advice, therefore, is to pass horses with plenty of room and at a speed which doesn't startle the horse. It may be tempting, if you see a horse up ahead and a nice clear overtaking opportunity, to just move offside and pass the horse wide, but without losing any speed. I cannot recommend this approach – you may pass the horse with enough room that the pass feels safe, but it's the sudden appearance of a fast-moving car in the horse's peripheral vision which will startle it, so it's important – even if you've a good, clear view past the horse – to slow down to a low speed when you pass it. Wait until you can see the horse in your centre rear-view mirror before pulling back in – this will ensure you're far enough ahead of the horse before you go back to the nearside. As you accelerate away, try to do it smoothly and progressively, rather than harshly.

Failed to signal or misleading signal   2%

We use signals when we're driving primarily as a way to let other road users know what we intend to do & there are a wider range of signals than you might think. Indicators, of course, headlight flash, horn, brake lights, reversing lights, hazard lights and hand signals all exist primarily so that we can let other road users know what we're about to do.

So it's important – if there is someone around who *might* benefit from a signal – that we give a signal in plenty of time. The thing to remember is that it isn't just other drivers who might benefit from a signal. Cyclists, pedestrians and the whole range of other road users could benefit from knowing what your intentions are, and will use your signals as part of their driving plans.

If the car in front puts on a left indicator, the next thing you expect to see is brake lights coming on, the car to slow and then turn left ahead. If the driver doesn't indicate, it's likely that the braking and turning may catch you by surprise and you'll have to take some avoiding action.

Signals – by which I mean well timed, clear and unambiguous signals – are therefore a really important part of our everyday driving. They're our main communication device with everyone else. Our visible Twitter feed or Facebook wall.

The trouble is, though, that you need to be very careful not to mislead people with your signals. If you signal left on the approach to a junction, the other road users will expect you to turn left. They'll base their plans around your signal, so if you then do not turn left, it could – and often does – put them in a difficult position.

It's therefore very important that you only give signals when you intend to follow them and if you change your mind, it's often better to take a wrong turn, rather than go against the signal you're giving.

It's easy to mislead people unintentionally with your signals. If there are a series of junctions to the left and you intend to turn into one of them, you should not give your signal until you've passed the junction *before* the one that you want to take.

Other drivers

If you want to avoid being misled by other drivers' signals, you should teach yourself not to trust them. I don't mean you should completely mistrust every signal given by other road users – that would pretty much make signalling a pointless exercise. What I mean is that you should look for other clues that the driver is going to do what they're signalling they'll do.

For example, if you're waiting to turn left out of a T junction and you see a vehicle approaching from your right with a left indicator on, it's easy to assume they're turning left into your junction. But are they? Look for the other clues that they're going to turn – are they slowing down? Is the driver looking towards the junction? Is there another entrance or junction just past your junction which they might be turning in to?

Once the other clues back up their signal, then it may be safe to go, but if you only see the signal, with no other clues, then you should wait and make absolutely sure that they are turning before you set off.

Junction restart (moving off at junction)   2%

This contributory factor relates to a situation – commonly at a roundabout junction - when the driver behind thinks that the driver in front is going, looks to the right and thinks that they can also go themselves, and they then drive straight into the car in front because that driver has changed his or her mind and stopped whilst the driver behind was still looking right.

To avoid this situation, if you're in a line of traffic approaching a roundabout, watch the car in front very carefully. When they become the front car at the give way line, keep watching them (alongside your other observations) until they set off. Then keep watching them so that you are sure they are moving off before making your final decision to go. After a final look right, look ahead again *before* accelerating.

Also, try not to be hesitant when setting off. This will avoid the driver behind making the classic mistake if you change your mind. Be patient at the line if it's busy - when you do go it should be a positive move.

2. BEHAVIOUR OR INEXPERIENCE (25% OF ALL ACCIDENTS)

Driver/Rider careless, reckless or in a hurry 18%

One of the most stressful aspects of driving is being late for something. When I was a police officer, *the* most common excuse I used to hear when booking people for speeding was "I'm sorry, but I'm late."

"I'm late for work."

"I'm late home."

"I'm late for a meeting."

"I'm late for the gym."

"I'm late for a hospital appointment."

"I'm late, I'm late, for a very important date."

Unfortunately, after filling in my paperwork they would then be an *awful* lot later!

Being late *always* magnifies small delays into major problems and creates tension. If you're in no hurry to get somewhere and you get caught up in some roadworks, it's not really a problem, but if you've set off for work at the last minute, only to find that the motorway is closed because of an accident and there are 5 miles of stationary traffic, then your stress levels will understandably rise.

As your stress levels increase, you are far more likely to take risks that you wouldn't normally take, and that additional stress also brings with it a tendency to think more about your arrival and less about your actual driving. Police officers are notorious for this – there is a common phenomenon called "noble cause risk taking", in which emergency response drivers will take unnecessary risks because, in their view, the emergency they are attending is *worth* the risk.

The most obvious tip to suggest here is to give yourself more time, but I think you'd find that a little patronising to say the least, so at the risk of sounding like your dad, I won't press that point any further.

I think it's probably better to look at how to stop that additional stress from affecting your driving. I find that the best way to do that is just to accept that you're going to be late. These things happen, and getting stressed about it won't make the problem go away, or make the traffic move any faster. Make some phone calls*, let people know you're going to be late, and then just take your time. If you're unexpectedly delayed during a journey, and you decide to "try and make it", you're far more likely to start taking risks, and risks, at any level, are something you should avoid at all costs.

A colleague of mine died in a road accident which occurred because he was driving too fast on a corner, lost control and hit an oncoming lorry. The reason he was driving too fast? He was a few minutes late for work because he'd set off, forgotten his lunch, and nipped back home to pick it up.

He left his wife a widow and his children fatherless, just because he was trying to make up a few minutes to meet a deadline which wasn't really that important in the grand scheme of things.

As a manager, I'd much prefer my staff to turn up for work a few minutes late, than have them take unnecessary risks to turn up on time. Ask your boss – I bet they'll agree with me!

Find a "happy place" in your mind – imagine you're on the beach, or skiing, and when the traffic starts moving again, think about your driving, and not about the time.

*Please note – I do not condone use of a mobile phone, hands-free or otherwise, whilst driving a car. Pull over somewhere safe to make your telephone calls!

Learner or inexperienced driver/rider   4%

Can you remember what it was like to be behind the controls of a car for the first time? And the first time you drove in traffic? Remember the nerves? The doubt? The almost overwhelming overload of things to remember and skills that you hadn't mastered?

Even for those of you who have only been driving a short time, it's difficult to think back to a time when you couldn't operate a cars controls or negotiate a straightforward junction or roundabout without having someone next to you telling you exactly what to do. Once you've been driving for a while, the actions become second-nature and you need to give very little – if any – thought to how you operate the controls or move the car down the road.

Because it's so easy to forget, I think it would do every experienced driver some good to spend a little time supervising a learner driver. When you're supervising a learner, you have to do all their thinking for them – and not just their thinking. You have to think *ahead* of them so that you can tell them what to do & how to operate the controls *before* they actually need to do it. It's not easy and I have to admit, even though I was a police driving instructor, I find teaching learners particularly stressful and I have nothing but respect for people who do it for a living.

If you want to supervise a learner, you don't need any special qualifications (unless you want to charge for your services) – you just need to be over 21 and have held a full drivers licence for a minimum of 3 years. So if you have a friend or relative who wants to practice their driving, you can accompany them in a suitably insured car and help them practice.

They key, though, is that you're helping them *practice*. Most learners these days will take a series of lessons from an approved driving instructor. In my opinion it's the only way to learn properly - ADIs are fully trained in providing instruction to learners, mostly in dual-control cars, and they're up-to-date with driving test procedure and everything else you need to learn before taking your test.

So as a "supervising" driver, you should bear in mind that your learner will be receiving structured lessons from their ADI which will bring them – over time – up to the standard required for test. This means that you should bear one overriding principle in mind if you're supervising a learner driver:

Don't try to change anything!

Your learner may not be driving in the way that you were taught, or in the way that you think is best – they may not, for instance, change down through the gears as they slow down in the same way that you do – but that's because their instructor has taught them the basics which will get them through their test.

They're already overloaded with information – particularly if they've only just started driving – and asking them to change something because you don't agree with their instructor is likely to cause them some serious problems.

The next time they have a lesson, it's likely that the instructor will spend half the lesson trying to undo the changes you've made! So just remember – you're there to supervise them and make sure they stay safe, but don't try to change anything that their instructor has taught them – it's highly likely that the instructor knows how to teach them much better than you do!

When you're out driving yourself, it's always good to know that inexperienced learner drivers are obliged to put notices on their car telling everyone that they are new to driving and likely to make mistakes. Along with "Taxi" signs, "L" plates are one of the most useful clues that the driver is likely to do something unexpected or make a silly mistake!

So you should always treat learner drivers with an element of caution. Don't get too close in traffic as they may stall or even roll back. Don't expect their use of the controls to be smooth and predictable – they may press the brakes sharply or react to something in front of them by braking or swerving more than is absolutely necessary.

Remember how stressful it was when you were learning and you stalled at a set of traffic lights? Becoming impatient or sounding your horn only adds to the learner's stress levels, and when they're stressed, they are more likely to continue the error and stall again, and again. Be patient with them, allow them to take their time, and you'll probably find that you'll make better progress than if you put pressure on them.

Aggressive driving   3%

Dealing with anger and aggression

This section was originally written as a short article for newly-qualified drivers. I re-edited it to fit the context of this book, but it just didn't read as well for some reason, so I've used the original version. I'm sure many of you have been driving for many years, but the advice in this section is just as relevant to someone who has been driving for 50 years, as it is to someone who passed their test yesterday...

If you're out shopping and someone walks into you accidentally, or steps into your path forcing you to step around them, what happens?

In a very British way, everyone apologises profusely to everyone else, we generally smile at each other, shrug and carry on with our shopping.

But out on the road, things change – dramatically.

Inside the protective environment of a car, many people's behaviour changes beyond recognition. Pull out accidentally in front of some people when they're driving, and they seem to become psychotic, aggressive animals. It never ceases to amaze me how a normally mild-mannered and polite person can change their personality so dramatically just by sitting in the driving seat of a car.

I used to have a dog that, when I took it out for a walk, would become ridiculously aggressive towards a neighbour's dog when it was safely locked behind a gate. The two of them would bark and snarl and growl at each other through the bars of the gate and you would have thought that, given the slightest opportunity, they would rip each other to pieces.

However, whenever my neighbour was out walking his dog, the two dogs would meet politely, sniff each other's bums, wag their tails and generally act like the friendly dogs they were.

It was only the presence of the gate which made them feel like they were safely separated, so they could play the big, hard dog routine.

Many drivers are the same. Behind a windscreen and steering wheel, they are invincible beings, impervious to any threats and aggressive in the extreme. If you walked past them in a supermarket, however, or saw them in a pub, they wouldn't say boo to a goose.

As a learner driver, you will already have experienced some aggression occasionally from other road users. You'll have stalled in front of someone who may have then blared their horn or pulled out in front of someone by mistake and received a headlight flash or a fist shake.

Generally, however, because you've been driving a car with "L" plates displayed, accompanied by an instructor or a qualified driver, other drivers will have given you a little leeway because you were a learner. Most people – even the most aggressive drivers – are a little more understanding of mistakes made by learner drivers.

Now you've passed your test, however, you're going to be on equal terms with every other driver out there. You'll no longer be advertising the fact that you're an inexperienced driver, and to everyone else on the road, there is no obvious indication that you're a new driver.

So here's what you should expect...

If you make a minor mistake by, perhaps, pulling out in front of another vehicle or stalling at some lights or by changing lanes carelessly, you will receive an aggressive response from approximately 75% of other drivers (this isn't a scientific 75% by the way – just my estimate based on my own experience).

By "aggressive response", I mean that they will sound their horn, drive unnecessarily close to you, flash their lights, shake their fist, give you any number of other (non-highway code!) hand signals, and generally behave in a very arsy manner.

There are also a very small minority of drivers who may go even further by getting out of their vehicles when you come to a stop, approaching you and remonstrating with you through the window of your car. I should add that these types of incidents are *extremely* rare, but it's useful for you to be aware that these people are out there, and to know how to deal with these situations if they ever arise.

How to deal with other drivers' aggression

Here's my first tip – and it's probably the most useful tip I can give you for dealing with aggressive drivers...

Apologise!

If you've made a mistake and someone is being aggressive with you – apologise.

It sounds simple, doesn't it? But it's amazing how many people make a mistake, receive an aggressive response and then respond themselves by sticking up one or two fingers, slamming on their brakes in front of the other driver, or responding in some other, equally aggressive manner.

Wouldn't it be much better to just acknowledge you've made a mistake and hold your hand up to apologise to the other driver?

Acknowledging your mistake, and apologising for it takes almost all the heat out of the situation and most other drivers will see your apology and accept it without escalating their aggressive behaviour. It's what you'd do if you were walking along the street and you bumped into someone, so why not take the same approach when you're driving?

Once you've apologised, the next tip is to...

Ignore them.

Once you've given an apology, if you're still receiving aggression from another driver, just ignore them. Getting involved in any kind of argument or fist-shaking competition will only aggravate the situation and escalate the aggression from the other driver.

They may be making you feel very uncomfortable, but if you completely ignore the aggressive driver – give them no reaction whatsoever – they will very quickly go their own way and you'll be able to get on with your journey.

Lock your doors

I said that it was very rare for another driver to get out of their vehicle to challenge you, but it does occasionally happen.

To keep yourself safe, the best advice is to lock your car doors before you set off on your journey. Most cars have central locking these days (all the locks operate automatically with the key and a switch inside the car). Get into the habit of locking the doors every time you set off. Many modern cars even have a setting which automatically locks the cars doors for you when you set off – check your cars handbook and switch the function on if it's fitted.

And if anyone tries to talk you out of locking your car doors by telling you that *"you'll be locked in the car if you have an accident"*, tell them they're talking nonsense. The car's doors will open in the normal way if you have an accident and anyone else will be able to open the car from the outside. The doors will only lock whilst you're driving and will unlock if you switch off the ignition or if you have an accident.

Driving with your car doors locked will also protect you from any opportunistic thieves who may want to open your door and grab any valuables from your car.

If someone does approach you

If someone does approach your car in an aggressive manner, ignore them, keep your doors locked and your windows closed and drive away as soon as you possibly can. If you're actually being physically threatened by someone, use your mobile phone to dial 999 and ask for police assistance – remember that you're allowed to use your phone whilst driving if it is an emergency.

If another vehicle appears to be following you, drive to the nearest safe place – a police station would be perfect, but anywhere else where there are other people will be fine. A fire or ambulance station, a garage forecourt, a supermarket, shopping centre or anywhere else where there are other people present. The presence of other people will generally put off the aggressive driver and they are far more likely to leave you alone.

Please don't worry too much though – being approached or followed is *extremely* rare and the chances are so small that it shouldn't in any way put you off driving.

Learn from your mistakes

If you've been subject to an aggressive response from another driver, try to use it as a learning experience. You're at a point in your driving career where you're looking to increase your experience as much as possible. Building up your experience does not mean getting things right all the time – you need to make mistakes so that you can learn from them and change your driving to avoid making the same mistake again.

So, if something you have done has wound up another driver, have a think about what you did, make a mental note of the circumstances which led up to you making that mistake, try to spot the same circumstances when you next go for a drive, and change your approach so that you don't make the same mistake again.

So many people make the same mistakes over and over again without learning from them – you're better than that!

Mistakes happen, but if the same mistake continues to happen, you've got a driving fault which needs to be corrected.

Watch your own behaviour

We've talked about other people's behaviour, but what about your own? You're very quickly building up your driving experience at the moment and as well as making your own mistakes, you'll start to spot mistakes made by other drivers. Sometimes their mistakes will force *you* to brake or take some other evasive action to avoid an accident.

How should *you* react?

Well, you know how it makes you feel if someone else is aggressive towards you – don't be "that" idiot!

The best response is just to deal with the incident, avoid the accident, take whatever action is necessary to stay safe and then...

Just carry on with your journey.

The very best drivers I've sat alongside are able to take other people's mistakes completely in their stride without allowing it to bother them at all. They don't gesticulate, they don't swear, they don't even comment about the other driver – they just deal with it and move on.

In dealing with other people's mistakes, you should also carry out two simple mental processes:

1. Forgive them

2. Learn from their mistake

By forgive them, I mean that you should bear in mind that whatever mistake they've made is exactly that – *a mistake* – which means they haven't done it deliberately, and they definitely haven't done it to annoy you. That might be the outcome, but it wasn't their intention, so forgive them. (And yes – before you ask – you should still forgive them if they're behaving like a dick!)

And by learning from their mistake, you're continuing to build up that bank of experience we've already talked about, without having to make the mistake yourself!

Look at the mistakes other drivers make and use that knowledge in your driving plans so that you don't make the same mistake.

Tips for more experienced drivers

These are a few slightly more advanced tips for more experienced drivers - techniques I used to teach to protection drivers during the road phase of a security escort course:

Remain fully aware of what's happening 360 degrees around your car at all times. Never get lazy and keep practising good all-round observations.

If you think a vehicle is following you there are a few techniques you can use to confirm whether it is following you or not, and a couple of simple counter-surveillance techniques you can use to get rid of them if they are following you.

To check if you're being followed, one of the simplest techniques is just to pull over by the side of the road and stop. See if the suspect vehicle does the same, or if it passes you and continues with its journey.

Go around the block. Turn left, then left again, then left again and then back onto the road you were originally on. It's unlikely that anyone else would want to go around the same random block, so if they do, they may be following you.

In a similar way, carry out what we used to call a "reciprocal" at the next roundabout - go all the way around and then either double-back on yourself or do a 360 and carry on in your original direction. A vehicle following you won't necessarily know where you're heading and will follow you on your pointless circuit.

If you think you are being followed, it's good practice to try to get the following vehicle to pass you - either in traffic or by carrying out a 360 at a roundabout or by going round a short block.

Once the vehicle is in front of you, wait till it's passed a junction or roundabout exit and then turn off quickly to the left (or right if you drive on the left - it doesn't require you to wait for a break in traffic). Turn off again and take a random series of turns. Leave it 10 or 15 minutes before you resume your original route.

If you're concerned about being followed and you have a regular journey at regular times, take different routes on different days. Keep varying your routine and avoid - at all costs - doing the same route at the same time every day.

Drive legally and non-aggressively at all times and don't enter into any conflicts with other drivers or road users.

Driver/Rider nervous, uncertain or panic   2%

Do you remember when you were a learner? The nerves of your first few lessons? The stress when you stalled at a busy set of lights? The nerves every time you had to perform a hill start?

And what about when you first passed your test? Remember the tension during your first few unaccompanied journeys? The panic that set in the first few times you had to negotiate a busy town centre? On your own? At night?

Some people never actually get over those feelings and become stressed at the very thought of driving a car – even if they have been qualified to drive for many years.

You may be a newly qualified driver and reading this book to help you build your driving experience or knowledge. You may also be someone who has had a long break from driving and are nervous about getting back behind the wheel – or a regular driver who finds driving a stressful and nerve-wracking experience.

My best advice for nervous drivers is to think about the fact that every other car or vehicle contains a human being. Driving is a social activity – we interact with other people all the time when we're driving. Nervous drivers seem to forget this and just see the vehicles – if you remember that there is a human being behind the wheel of those vehicles, you're likely to feel much less stressed and nervous.

Take some time to get your seating position just right – so that you're comfortable and you have a good view out of the car. Avoid tensing up – try to keep your grip on the wheel fairly relaxed and don't clench your buttocks – this can lead to all sorts of back-and-bum aches and pains.

If you're feeling particularly stressed, take a short break, get away from the traffic and continue your journey once you've calmed down.

Unfamiliar with model of vehicle   1%

A small but significant number of accidents are, in part, attributed to drivers being unfamiliar with the model of vehicle they were driving at the time – 21 fatal accidents involved this contributory factor in 2014.

When I was in the police, swapping from vehicle to vehicle was second nature to me – I might be driving a Range Rover one minute and a Mercedes Sprinter van the next – it was just something I would do without giving it very much thought at all. Even now I can jump in a new (to me) car and drive it without giving very much thought to the differences in controls, drive and feel of the new car.

I am, however, acutely aware that this is not the case for the majority of people. Most people have access to one – or possibly two cars at the most and changing to a different car can be a stressful and often confusing business.

So I've thought carefully about what I do when I'm faced with a new car for the first time & how I familiarise myself with the controls:

I start by getting in and setting my seat & mirrors correctly so that I'm comfortable and have a good view out of and behind the car. Do this before you even start the engine (you may need the ignition switched on if the car has electrically-adjustable seats) so that you're not driving down the road with your chin on the steering wheel and your head brushing the roof whilst simultaneously trying to fiddle with the unfamiliar seat controls.

Then check that the handbrake or parking brake is on, check the car is in neutral (or "N" if it's an automatic), press the clutch (or brake in an auto) and start the engine without pressing the accelerator.

Let the dials settle down, check that all the warning lights – apart from the handbrake light – have gone off and then have a good look at the instruments, dials and controls. Do you know how to turn on the lights? Or the wipers? How do you operate the windscreen washers? And how do you set the heater/air conditioning so that the car isn't steaming up & you're comfortable?

These are all things that you should do before setting off, whilst the car is stationary. You don't want to be staring like a dummy at the overcomplicated climate control just as you're joining a motorway slip road with steamed-up windows. Neither do you want to be flapping about, trying to find out how to switch on the wipers as you're driving through an unexpected thunderstorm.

Have a play with the controls and make sure you know how to operate them before setting off. When you do need the wipers, you might have to think for half-a-second, but at least you'll know roughly what to do if you need them in a hurry.

When you do drive off, you should be aware that each and every car "feels" slightly different to drive. Even identical models can feel slightly different – the brakes will have a slightly different "bite" or the clutch will engage at a different point.

This difference in "feel" can catch out many drivers, so just take your time and get used to the feel of the clutch and the effectiveness of the brakes – some cars need only a tiny brush on the brake pedal to bring on very strong braking. Others need a fair old shove on the pedal before they start to work effectively. You don't want to be finding out how sensitive or otherwise your brakes are the first time you *really* need them, so find somewhere quiet and try the brakes a few times.

Avoid playing with stereos, radios, Bluetooth links, streaming audio and all other manner of in car entertainment whilst you're driving. Wait until you're stopped so that you're not distracted. Remember that, although having a new car is a novelty and you'll be really excited to play with all the gadgets and gizmos, you're still driving and it's your *driving* which needs your full attention.

Many people are intimidated if they move from a smaller car to a larger car. Don't be! Just take your time, drive on roads you're familiar with at first and get used to the size of the car. It's amazing how a car which looks large on the outside suddenly seems to shrink around you as soon as you start driving it.

Moving from a manual to an automatic for the first time catches many people out. Automatics are actually very easy and relaxing to drive – you've no clutch control to master, no gears to change yourself and there's just two pedals – "stop" and "go".

When driving an auto for the first time, remember to put your left foot on the footrest, or flat on the floor, and leave it there! You should never use your left foot for braking in an automatic car – if you try to press the brake pedal with your left foot, you'll just stomp it to the floor as though you're pressing the clutch and the car will stand on its nose, scaring your passengers and *really* scaring the following vehicles!

Instead, remember to only use your right foot for accelerating and braking.

When you start an automatic, do it with your right foot on the brake pedal and keep the brake pedal pressed whilst you shift into "D" or "Drive". The car will "creep" forward when you remove pressure from the brake pedal. They generally creep enough to allow you to do almost all of your low-speed manoeuvring, parking etc. using the brake pedal only.

If you're new to autos, stick it in drive and leave it there. Don't start messing around with sport settings and manual settings until you've got a feel for the new car. Automatics will do 99% of everything you want to do in Drive, so just use that setting for your first few drives.

If you're renting a left-hand drive car for the first time abroad, follow the above advice, but also get used to trying to change gear with the window-winder! I do it every time I drive a left-hooker, at least for the first day until I've mentally adjusted to driving cack-handed!

Left hand drive cars will have the controls laid out in exactly the same way as right-hand drive cars – clutch, accelerator & brake are all in the same position, just on the other side of the car so you shouldn't be intimidated by driving a left-hooker.

One other important thing you should be familiar with in a new car is which wheels are driven. Front-wheel drive cars, rear-wheel drive cars and four-wheel drive cars all have different handling characteristics and it's always useful to know which wheels are driven by the engine.

Inexperience of driving on the left   0% (429)

This is a relatively low figure, but foreign drivers can easily make the mistake of driving on the right when they're new to the country, so you should watch out for these drivers.

You're more likely to come across these drivers if you live near to a sea port or airport. The cars are easier to spot leaving a sea port as they'll generally be displaying foreign number-plates, but those driving away from airports are more difficult to spot and will generally be driving UK registered rental cars. Look out for late-model, clean cars, being driven with an element of hesitancy. Some will also have small stickers in the rear window advertising the rental company.

You should also be aware of these drivers if you live in a part of the country which is particularly popular for foreign tourists. The Scottish Highlands, for instance, The lake District, or Stratford-on-Avon. Watch for vehicles leaving hotels and guesthouses first thing in the morning, as this is when the drivers will be most likely to forget that we drive in the left in the UK.

If you do encounter a car on the wrong side of the road, slow down and be prepared to stop. Flash your lights to get their attention & sound your horn if you think it will help. There is a mental block period that these drivers go through – they will completely forget that they should be on the left and will actually be looking at cars driving towards the as though *they* are the idiots. It can sometimes take them some considerable time to realise that its *they* who are in the wrong!

If you're ever unlucky enough to encounter a vehicle travelling on the wrong side of a motorway, move into the lane furthest away from the one they're travelling in, or even the hard shoulder if necessary. It's thankfully pretty rare, but drivers on the wrong carriageway are usually confused or drunk – not foreign. they'll either drive on the hard shoulder or in the outside (2nd, 3rd or 4th lane, depending on the width of the motorway). With that in mind, your best course of action is to slow and drive in the middle lane – usually lane 2, or lane 1 on a two-lane motorway.

Driving too slow for conditions or slow vehicle (e.g. tractor)   0% (94)

Driving too slow – by which I mean driving *well* below the posted speed limit for no good reason can be just as dangerous as driving too fast. Some drivers think the slower they go the safer they'll be, but they fail to take into account the frustration – and sometimes aggression – that this can cause in other road users. If you drive too slowly on a generally fast road, other drivers will often be taken by surprise if they're not expecting a vehicle to be travelling slowly and this can be hazardous.

If there are no obvious hazards and conditions are good, you should aim to drive at, or close to the posted speed limit for the road or vehicle that you're driving. We drive to get to places, and we should be making reasonable progress where appropriate, so that we're not holding up traffic unnecessarily or causing frustration.

Frustrated drivers will take risks and look to overtake where it's not appropriate, or where it's dangerous to do so.

If, for whatever reason (faulty car, for instance, or towing a heavy load), you have to drive at low speed, keep a careful eye on what's happening behind. To avoid causing unnecessary frustration, look for somewhere safe to pull over every now and again, to let the following vehicles pass you safely without taking risks.

If you're behind a slow-moving vehicle, by all means, overtake it! But do it when it's safe and clear and you're not likely to come into conflict with other road users. I've covered overtaking in great detail in my book "Advanced & Performance Driving", so if you want to learn more about the dark art of overtaking, get yourself a copy!

If you're not comfortable with overtaking another vehicle, don't sit really close to the back of it. If you do, you're creating a much longer "vehicle" for those behind to overtake. Instead, drop back and leave a reasonable gap in case the people behind want to overtake, so that, if necessary, they can pass you first, pull in, and then overtake the slow-moving vehicle ahead. If someone behind does decide to overtake, don't accelerate to close the gap in front of you – this can be extremely dangerous for the overtaking vehicle and the oncoming vehicles.

3. INJUDICIOUS ACTION (23% OF ALL ACCIDENTS)

"Injudicious Action" seems like a bit of an old-fashioned, anachronistic term to me. I imagine a dusty old judge sat in a stuffy courtroom passing judgement. "You are hereby convicted of two counts of injudicious action. I sentence you to six months' penal servitude and a week in the stocks".

In reality, "injudicious actions" are basically just "bad decisions". Not careless actions which have been carried out accidentally or without any intent, but actions which a driver has *decided* to do – even if they know they shouldn't.

So let's look at them in order and see what you can do to avoid having one of these accidents.

Travelling Too Fast for Conditions   7%

This sits at the top of the list, being involved in 7% of all accidents (7,737 accidents in the UK in 2014).

I'm going to start by stating clearly what this contributory factor is *not.*

It's not speeding.

By which I mean it isn't exceeding the speed limit – I'll deal with that later in this chapter. No – this contributory factor is more specific (and causes more accidents than speeding) in that it refers to drivers travelling *too fast for the conditions.*

Let's start by looking at the difference between speeding and travelling too fast for the conditions.

On a clear, dry day, in light traffic, I may choose to travel at 75mph on the motorway. The national speed limit on the motorway in the UK is 70mph, so in those circumstances I'd be exceeding the speed limit – speeding. It's unlikely that I'll have an accident, to be honest, and no kittens will be killed in the process, but I'll be committing an offence and I could potentially be prosecuted for speeding.

On a different day, however, on the same motorway, it's very foggy and visibility is down to 50 metres or so. On this day I choose to drive at 70mph, so I'm not speeding. However, the overall stopping distance at 70mph is 96 metres, so if I suddenly come across stationary traffic, there is no way that I'll be able to stop safely without hitting it.

In these circumstances I'd be travelling too fast for the conditions.

It doesn't just have to be fog, or reduced visibility – any number of different conditions could make certain speeds too fast. Ice or frost on the road surface, for example, or an oil or fuel spillage. Just a wet road can be slippery at times, or a poorly maintained road surface. Darkness, poor lighting, a low sun on the horizon blinding you, standing water and a multitude of other conditions.

The overriding principle you should bear in mind when deciding how fast to travel at is this:

You should always be able to stop, on your own side of the road, in the distance you can see to be clear.

This is an old advanced driving principle, but it's just as true today and should always be at the back of your mind when you're driving.

The question "could I stop?" should always be in your mind when you're behind the wheel. Could I stop if that car pulls out in front of me? Could I stop if that dog ran out? Could I stop if the car in front stops suddenly, without warning? Could I stop if I suddenly and unexpectedly want a pie from that shop?

When it comes to deciding on what speed to travel at, all these thoughts, and hundreds more, will be going through your mind and one of the primary considerations should be "what are the road and weather conditions like?"

Don't just assume that, because the speed limit for a road is 30, 40, 50, 60 or 70 mph, that it's always safe to travel at those speeds. Don't see the speed limit as a target – use your judgement to choose your speed and always take the conditions into account.

If you think you couldn't stop safely because of the poor visibility, road surface or weather conditions, then you're travelling too fast. Slow down a little until you're comfortable that you *could* stop safely if you needed to.

One thing which never ceases to amaze me is that people will go out of their house on a cold, icy morning and spend 10 minutes scraping a thick layer of frost and ice from the windscreen and windows of their car so that they can see clearly to drive. They'll then get in their car and drive like they always do – as though the road is dry and the weather is warm – completely ignoring the fact that, if their car is iced up, there's a really good chance that the road will be icy too.

This sounds like simple common sense, but when you've got in your car on a cold day and the heater has warmed up, it's easy to forget just how cold it is outside.

I've mentioned fog briefly, but one of the most difficult and hazardous driving conditions is patchy fog. When fog is thick and consistent, people will generally reduce their speed and drive more carefully. Unfortunately, fog doesn't always behave in such a predictable way and will sometimes appear as thick fog patches.

You may be driving along in good, clear visibility and then suddenly drive into a fog patch or fog bank which you weren't expecting. The problem here is that your speed may have been perfectly safe before you drove into the fog bank, but then, suddenly, your speed will be too fast for the visibility.

Slowing down may seem to be the sensible option in these circumstances, but the danger in slowing is that the vehicles behind you may not be able to see you and appreciate that you're slowing. This is how patchy fog can cause multiple-vehicle pile-ups on motorways and other fast roads.

If there is a likelihood of encountering patchy fog, or if one patch of fog catches you out (bearing in mind that you're then highly likely to encounter further fog patches), then reduce your speed whilst the visibility is good and other people can see you. You can then maintain this lower speed through both the fog patches and the clear visibility between them. If your speed is consistent (and appropriate), there is also far less chance that other drivers will fail to see you.

Fog patches can linger after a wider bank of fog has lifted, so be aware of the areas where fog can hang around – in dips in the road or other low-lying areas and around water – where bridges pass over rivers, canals and estuaries.

Another issue which can catch drivers out and make them find that, suddenly, their speed is too high for the conditions, is the issue of microclimates.

"Microclimates" are areas along the road where the conditions aren't – for various reasons – consistent with the rest of the road you're driving along.

For example, on a bright winters morning, the rising sun will thaw any frost or ice which has been lying on the road surface. That will mean that the road will thaw and will just be damp, or even dry an hour or so after sunrise. The microclimate, however, will be the areas in the shade which the sun hasn't been able to reach – alongside high walls, under the shade of trees, bridges etc. In these areas, there is a much higher chance that the road will still be frosty or icy and there is, therefore, a real danger that the speed which was appropriate for the dryer, thawed stretches of road, will, actually, be much too high for the icy patches which remain in the shaded areas.

Another example: after rainfall on a warm day, the road will dry quite quickly, leaving a nice, dry and grippy road surface. In areas of the road which have overhanging trees, however, the trees will prevent the road from drying as quickly and will retain water which will continue to drip onto the road surface, so, again, speeds which were appropriate for the dry stretch of road, may not be appropriate for the corner which is sheltered by overhanging trees.

Microclimates can hide in some less obvious places too – on a windy day, you may be comfortable with a crosswind on an exposed motorway and you may be dealing with it nicely by applying some pressure on the steering wheel to counter the crosswind. Pull alongside a large lorry, however, and you're suddenly sheltered from the wind. Keep the pressure on the wheel and you'll feel as though you're being "sucked" towards the lorry.

Ask anyone who rides a motorbike about this one – they'll tell you how scary it can be!

Following too close   7%

7% of accidents are caused by people following each other too closely.

If I'm being honest, I thought this figure would be much higher. Rear-end shunt type accidents are very common, particularly in today's heavy traffic and I would have guessed the figure to have been closer to 20% rather than just 7%.

I think the reason it's not higher is that the majority of rear-end shunts take place at relatively low speeds and don't result in injuries. Remember that the available figures only relate to injury accidents which are attended by the police, and it's likely that the majority of minor rear-end shunts are not reported to the police or attended by an officer.

Irrespective of the reasons for the underreporting, it's really important that you understand the reasons why these types of accident happen & what you can do to avoid them. Remember that, even if you're not injured, any accident is a real pain in the arse and can leave you out of pocket, out of car and severely cheesed off!

Tailgating

By far the most common reason for rear-end shunts is (and I apologise if I'm stating the bleeding obvious!) - people drive too close to the vehicle in front!

Tailgating, in other words.

You know the type of driving I'm talking about. If you've ever driven on British roads, you'll have experienced someone so close behind that you can make out the individual hairs on their chin in your rear-view mirror. They look like they're sat on your back seat. It's a very common driving fault committed by an extremely high number of drivers on a daily basis.

The other problem is that – despite the high number of accidents caused by driving too close – *most of the time* people tailgate, they *don't* have an accident. In other words, they usually get away with it, so their tailgating *usually* goes unpunished and they generally don't learn from it.

Why is tailgating a problem?

It's an issue for a number of reasons. Firstly, if you're driving too close to the vehicle in front and it brakes suddenly, without warning, it's highly unlikely that you'll realise what is happening, decide what to do, move your foot from the accelerator to the brake and then press the brake hard enough, quickly enough to stop without hitting the vehicle in front.

So, drive too close and you'll struggle to stop if the car in front stops suddenly.

Secondly, the closer you get to the vehicle in front, the more it fills your field of vision. In other words, if you're only a few feet from the back of a lorry, you'll only really be able to see the lorry, with a bit of road passing by in your peripheral vision.

So you won't be able to see what's happening in front of the lorry, whether the traffic ahead is flowing or slowing, whether there is an obstruction ahead of the lorry or whether something is about to pull out in front of the lorry, possibly causing it to stop suddenly without warning...

And then we're back to the first problem.

In other words, if you're so close to the vehicle in front that you can't see, you won't spot when they're going to brake and you'll struggle to stop if they stop suddenly.

Thirdly, if you're too close to the vehicle in front, and at the same time the vehicle *behind* is too close, your braking will be sudden and harsh and there is a much higher chance that the car behind will rear-end you.

So you could be shunted up the rear as well as in front. That'll make your eyes water!

On a slight aside before I go any further, have you ever been travelling along the motorway in heavy traffic and the traffic ahead comes to a stop, before moving off a minute or so later without any apparent cause? Traffic stops, traffic moves off again, but there's no accident, no obstruction, no reason for everything to stop? Have you ever wondered what's going on?

It happens because so many people drive too close to the car in front in heavy traffic on the motorway.

A vehicle ahead brakes ever so slightly, but because the vehicle behind it is travelling too close, the driver has to brake *just slightly* harder than the first one. The one behind is also too close, so they have to brake *ever so slightly* harder, and the one behind has to brake a little harder etc. etc.

Within a few seconds, this effect has rippled back through the following traffic until the cars 30 or 40 back are braking very hard and eventually coming to a stop before moving off again quite quickly.

Go back a few hundred cars and this can multiply into traffic stopping, sometimes for several minutes, with no discernible reason. If people left a reasonable distance from the vehicle in front, this would never happen!

How close should I follow the vehicle in front?

Sorry, but there's no simple answer to this question – it depends on a couple of main factors.

How fast are you travelling, and how big is the vehicle in front?

A good following position from the vehicle in front will allow you a good view of the road ahead – and ahead of the vehicle in front – so that you can plan for what's coming up and for what is going to make the vehicle in front slow, or alter its course.

So if you're behind a motorcycle, you'll have a good view around it because it doesn't take up much room on the road, whereas if you're behind a lorry, you'll need to be much further back to get a good view around it.

As for speed, the first question you should be asking is (as with the previous section) could I stop?

If the car in front brakes hard without warning, could you react in time and stop without running into it? If the answer is no, then you're too close!

The other thing to consider is whether you're making it safer for following vehicles. If the vehicle in front *does* brake sharply, it's better to be a bit further back so that you don't need to brake as sharply. If you don't need to brake as sharply, neither will the car behind – even if they're tailgating – and there's less chance of them collecting you as a bonnet ornament.

The most common advice dished out by advanced driving types (myself included!) is to maintain a following distance of at least 2 seconds from the vehicle in front. The distance is expressed in seconds, rather than distance, because you need to take into account the fact that following distances need to be much longer at higher speeds.

At 30 mph, you're travelling at 44 feet per second and your braking distance is 45 feet.

At 60mph, you're travelling at 88 feet per second, but your braking distance isn't doubled – it's quadrupled! To 180 feet.

So the faster you're travelling, the further back you should be from the vehicle in front.

To calculate a two second gap, wait till the vehicle in front passes something stationary – a road marking, for instance, or a bridge, and start counting (out loud if you like! I do it in my head these days though, as it usually spooks my passengers) "ONE THOUSAND AND ONE, ONE THOUSAND AND TWO".

If you don't get to two before you pass the road marking or pass under the bridge, then you're less than two seconds behind & you're too close. Slow down a little, back off and try it again a minute later.

You've probably all heard the old saying "only a fool breaks the two second rule".

It's rubbish.

It's rubbish because it's not a rule – two seconds is often not the appropriate following position and you should sometimes drop back much further. If it's icy, for instance, or the road surface is slippery, it will obviously take you longer to stop in an emergency, so you should at least double your following position. Much more if it's icy. And if you're behind a large lorry or bus, you should drop back to 4 or 5 seconds so that you can keep a good view of the road ahead.

You can also (occasionally) get a little closer than 2 seconds. If you're looking to overtake, you can get a little closer (down to 1 ½ seconds) on right-hand corners where there might be an opportunity to overtake. Don't forget to drop back, though if the overtake isn't on.

So 2 seconds is not a rule, but it is a reasonable guideline if you're following another car in good visibility on a decent road surface.

What about when other drivers are tailgating me?

So we've looked at how to avoid being a tailgater yourself, but what should you do if someone is tailgating *you?* They're right up your arse! What's wrong with them? Haven't they read Reg's book? Don't they know how dangerous it is? What do they want me to do?

Firstly, don't take it personally – many people get extremely intimidated by tailgating drivers, but it's not personal – they probably don't even know they're doing it & they definitely don't know how risky their driving is.

But *you* do – so there are a few sensible things you can do – and avoid doing - to make sure they don't run up your rear.

Firstly, don't brake-test them. If you've got someone seemingly hooked on to your rear bumper it can be very tempting to take the rise and give them a taste of their own medicine by dabbing your brakes in an attempt to get them to back off. I've seen it loads of times – the driver in front takes offence at the tailgater and then makes the situation immediately far more dangerous by suddenly braking without warning.

At worst, they'll drive into your boot. At best, you're likely to get an aggressive reaction from the driver behind, which could lead to all kinds of shenanigans, so brake testing should be avoided at all costs.

If the vehicle behind is too close, the first thing you should do is extend your own following distance from the car in front of *you*. If you drop back, you'll be able to brake much more gently if the car in front brakes, and then there will be less likelihood of the vehicle behind you failing to brake in time.

If you need to brake for a hazard of to turn off, start braking earlier than you would normally – if you just gently rest your foot on the brake pedal for a couple of seconds before pressing it, you'll activate your brake lights without actually braking and the tailgater will hopefully realise you're slowing and avoid hitting you.

If you're driving along at a speed you're happy with and you've acquired a tailgater who's been there for some time, ease off the accelerator & slow a little to see if they choose to overtake you – it's often better to have the idiot in front of you where you can see them, rather than behind you where they could do anything!

If they don't pass, stick a left indicator on and pull over until they do pass you. It never ceases to amaze me how reluctant these type of drivers can be to overtake and a good proportion will continue along at your speed after passing you. You'd think they would want to disappear off into the distance at warp speed after sitting aggressively on your bumper for 10 miles, but as I previously mentioned, many of them don't know they're doing it and will merrily trundle along at their previous speed after passing you!

So keep your distance and watch what's happening behind – it could avoid you being the unwilling meat in a very unpleasant sandwich!

Exceeding speed limit   5%

This was a very surprising statistic – only 5% of accidents have "exceeding the speed limit" as a contributory factor.

When you consider how much road safety policy and advice concentrates on speeding, and how heavily enforced speed limits are becoming, you'd think, wouldn't you, that people were being killed and maimed at a biblical level by hundreds of thousands of irresponsible speeding motorists?

But no – only 5% of all accidents – 5,309 reportable accidents (out of a total of 115,673 a year) are caused in part by speeding motorists.

Having said that, the percentage of *fatal* accidents caused by speeding is much higher. 16% of fatalities a year are caused in part by speeding – 254 fatal accidents (out of a total of 1,543).

There are some good reasons why these statistics look like this. Firstly, in the vast majority of accidents (resulting in minor injuries) the police officer attending the scene will only have the word of the participants to go off when deciding on what contributory factors to choose.

I cannot tell you how many accidents I attended during my police career where utter carnage has been caused by someone who was "only doing about 25mph, officer". It's nonsense, of course, and it's obvious to anyone with half a brain that they *were* speeding and that they're lying, but the police don't have the resources to fully investigate every single accident which occurs, carry out skid tests, plan out the scene and calculate approximate speeds of vehicles involved.

In the vast majority of cases, officers will not have any substantial evidence of speeding, and so they'll not tick the "exceeding speed limit" box.

In the cases of fatal accidents, however – and some serious accidents – these resources *are* available. Specialist accident investigators will attend the scene with their calculators and huge brains and eventually work out approximate speeds of the vehicles involved in the accident.

So it's likely that the *true* figure for all accidents is much closer to the figure of 16% for fatal accidents.

Because we're all liars.

So what's the big deal with speed limits? I've always maintained that if everyone – *everyone* – drove at a speed which is appropriate to the road, traffic and weather conditions all the time, there would be no need whatsoever for speed limits.

Travelling at 30mph outside a school, for instance, at 3.15 on a weekday, may be much too fast, even if it's the posted speed limit.

On the other hand, (whilst in proud possession of a legal exemption from speed limits) I have travelled at speeds well in excess of 150mph on public roads perfectly safely, despite speed limits of 60 or 70mph being in force.

The problem with this theory, of course, is that – as you're probably aware - some people are idiots, and once those idiots started using their free choice and driving at inappropriate speeds with no fear of the consequences, accidents would quickly rise – particularly in busy, urban areas.

So we have speed limits which, on the whole, although they're aimed at the lowest common denominator, are usually at least a good indicator of the number of hazards you'll encounter on a particular road. So a road with a 20mph speed limit will generally be in a heavily built-up area with lots of pedestrians, children etc., whereas a road with a 60mph national speed limit will generally be out in a more rural area with less roadside hazards, where it would be safer to travel at a higher speed.

Another thing to bear in mind whilst we're examining speeding and speed limits is that almost all accidents do not occur at, or even anywhere near the posted speed limit.

Before an accident happens, there is a moment in time when all the drivers involved try to do something – anything – to avoid the accident.

I call it the "OH SHIT!" moment.

It's the moment which occurs between the point when you realise an accident is definitely going to happen, and the accident actually happening.

The OH SHIT! moment can last anywhere from a fraction of a second up to perhaps 15 or 20 seconds depending on the circumstances, but irrespective of the length of the OH SHIT! Moment, drivers usually manage to do something – brake.

It's an instinctive reaction for any driver – just press the brakes and slow down as much as possible – and it's a good reaction, to be honest.

But because of this reaction, as I've already mentioned, accidents do not normally occur at the speed limit – or usually anywhere near them. People may think "I was travelling at 40mph when the accident happened, so I had the accident at 40mph", but in reality, because of the OH SHIT! moment, they will have braked hard and reduced their speed to maybe 15 or 20mph before the accident happened.

Now, don't get me wrong – a 15 or 20mph impact can be quite jarring and people can suffer injuries as a result, but a *genuine* 40mph impact can actually be devastating, depending on the circumstances.

So where does this lead to with speed limits? Well, if you're in a 30mph speed limit area and you're travelling at 45mph when a child steps out in front of you, your OH SHIT! moment will allow you to lose maybe 15mph before hitting the child, resulting in a 30mph impact.

Now, studies have shown that pedestrians hit by a car travelling at 30mph have a 50% chance of dying. So this scenario results in a 50% possibility that the child will die. Even if the child lives, they're likely to suffer serious, life-changing injuries.

If, however, you're on the same road at the same time, but you choose to drive at or around the 30mph speed limit, the OH SHIT! moment when the child steps out will still result in you losing perhaps 15mph, but because your *starting* speed was 30, rather than 45, you'll hit the child at 15mph, rather than 30.

Those same studies have shown that pedestrians hit by a car travelling at less than 20mph have a 10% chance of dying. Or, in other words, a 90% chance of living – and probably with much less serious injuries too.

What I'm trying to say is that speed limits aren't just there to keep you safe – you could speed all day every day for years without losing control or having an accident. Rather, speed limits are there to protect other, more vulnerable road users.

They're not even there to *prevent* accidents either. The vast, *vast* majority of accidents occur well below the posted speed limit (partly due to the OH SHIT! moments). They are there, however, in an attempt to ensure that, when accidents *do* happen, they result in less deaths and serious injuries.

So, be aware of the speed limits, be aware that they're lower in areas where there are more hazards, look out for those increased hazards when you're in lower speed limit areas and try to be sensible.

There is a time and a place for faster driving and it's away from residential areas, out in the countryside, where there is less traffic, less pedestrians and the roads are more enjoyable.

Disobeyed 'Give Way' or 'Stop' sign or markings 3%

This contributory factor accounts for 3% of all accidents in the UK – approximately 3500 accidents per year or 10 per day.

Let's start by looking at the difference between the two signs/markings.

"**Give Way**" means that you should give priority to other vehicles on a major road. You'll see give way markings at junctions where you're on a minor road and joining a more major road, or at a roundabout, where you should be giving priority to vehicles which are approaching from the right.

You'll usually see a triangular "Give Way" sign on the approach to the junction, a large inverted triangle painted on the road surface just before the junction and two sets of dotted white lines across the end of the junction where it meets the major road or roundabout – this is the "Give Way" line. You may also sometimes see the words "Give Way" painted on the road surface.

So what does "Give Way" mean? Well, it doesn't necessarily mean you have to stop, but it does mean that anything on the major road, or approaching from the right on the roundabout, has priority over you. That means you should let them pass and wait for a suitable gap before you pull out.

It's not exactly rocket science, is it? But it never ceases to amaze me how many people either fail to grasp the meaning of "Give Way", or simply choose to ignore it because they've been waiting at the junction for ages and the traffic is heavy and their journey is far more important than yours so f#*% it, I'm pulling out! You'll have to brake!

Firstly, if you've been waiting at a junction for ages and the traffic is heavy and no-one is letting you out, the only correct approach is to...

Wait for it...

No – that's it – you should wait for it – for a suitable gap. Waiting is something we're not very good at in the UK, but wait you must – you don't suddenly inherit some priority over other vehicles just because you've been waiting for a couple of minutes – a delay in your journey doesn't give you permission to pull out on other vehicles.

If you're waiting at a junction and the traffic is busy, stop with your wheels at the line (I avoid creeping forwards) and try to get eye contact with the drivers on the main road. Winding your window down often helps. Look relaxed and friendly and very soon someone will let you out. Give them a smile and a thumbs up and set off briskly.

This is the social aspect of driving in busy traffic. The part which involves genuine personal interaction with human beings. Give a little and take a little.

If the major road you're approaching *isn't* particularly busy, you can join it at a give way junction without stopping. At roundabouts in particular, you may have a really good view on the approach and be able to plan your entry to the roundabout without necessarily coming to a complete stop – or sometimes without even having to slow too much.

It's called "planning to stop, but looking to go". So on the approach to a roundabout or other give way junction, your plan should be to stop at or before the give way lines, but if, as you get closer to the junction, you can see that it's clear or there is a suitable gap, you should come off the brakes and go if it's safe to do so.

This approach keeps the traffic flowing nicely and prevents frustration from the vehicles behind who might not be expecting you to stop.

"**Stop**" means one thing and one thing only. If you can't work out what it means, perhaps you're a little hard of thinking, but just in case, I'll spell it out for you.

At a "Stop" sign you should...

Stop.

The markings for a "Stop" junction are different to those for a "Give Way" junction. Firstly, the sign at, or on the approach to the junction will be a red octagonal sign with "Stop" in bold letters. The word "Stop" will usually be written in large letters on the road surface just before the junction and at the junction itself will be a single, thick, solid white line – this is the "Stop" line.

"Stop" markings and signs are usually used at junctions which have a very limited view of the major road. So the road planners have examined these junctions carefully and decided that "Give Way" isn't appropriate – the view for drivers approaching the junction is so poor that the only safe way to emerge from the junction is by stopping first, looking carefully, and then emerging when it's clear.

As I mentioned earlier, the one thing you *must* do at a "Stop" junction is stop. By which I mean, you must come to a complete, stationary, non-moving, motionless, static, immobile stand-still. You must stop.

It never ceases to amaze me how many people fail to stop at "Stop" signs. They slow right down, of course – down to a very slow crawl as they approach the junction – but then roll slowly over the stop line without actually stopping.

I've sat next to police officers on driving courses and watched them do this. When I challenge them about it, they don't even realise – they think they've stopped, but they haven't!

The way driving instructors tackle this issue is by asking their students to stop and apply the handbrake at every stop sign. This means that the driver can be absolutely sure that they've come to a stop before moving off again and they won't fail their test if they encounter a "Stop" junction.

As a result, many people believe that it's a legal requirement to apply your handbrake at a "Stop" junction, but it's not. The only legal requirement is that you stop. That means that if you come to a stop on your footbrake – a complete stop, mind you – and the road you're joining is clear, you can move off without applying your handbrake. But if you're in any doubt, stick to the handbrake rule – it might save you three points or, more relevantly, it might just stop you from having an accident, which is, of course, why you bought this book in the first place!

Other drivers

So that's you sorted then – you know you should stop or give way depending on the signs and road markings, but what about everyone else? How do you deal with drivers who *don't* stop or give way where they should do?

The secret is in using your imagination.

When you're driving down the road and there are a number of junctions, entrances and driveways up ahead, you should imagine that, just out of view, there are loads of drivers in vehicles just waiting to pull out in front of you.

There aren't of course, but if you imagine that there are, you'll move away from these junctions as you approach them – towards the centre of the road. Moving towards the centre of the road has two advantages. Firstly, it allows you to see a little further into the junctions up ahead. Secondly, it allows any drivers in those junctions to see you a little earlier. Not much, but a bit, and sometimes you only need a little bit of an advantage to prevent an accident.

So, assume there is someone hidden in every junction, waiting to pull out and move towards the centre-line to give yourself (and them) a better, earlier view.

If you do see a vehicle pull up to a junction up ahead, there are a few little things you should be looking for. Have a look at the driver – are they looking in your direction? Or are they just looking straight ahead or to their left? Can they see you? Have you got some form of "eye contact" with them, or are they messing with their phone, scolding their children or picking their nose? The driver who looks at you is less likely to pull out than the ones who are doing the other things.

Secondly, look at the cars wheels. Are they stationary? Or are they turning? If they're turning, are they still slowing down as they approach the junction, or are they starting to speed up as the driver starts to "go". If the wheels are stationary when you first see the vehicle and they then start to turn, the driver may well be about to pull out.

Thirdly, if you can see the rear of the vehicle, you may well be able to see the brake lights. If the brake lights are on, the driver has their foot on the brake pedal and are less likely to pull out than if the brake lights are off. If you can see the brake lights illuminated and they then go off, the driver is almost certainly about to set off, so be careful!

If you're picking up these clues that someone is about to pull out, don't just wait for them to do it! Do something! Now!

Slow down, move as far away from the junction as you can and be prepared to stop. If the car is still in the junction, you might want to give them a horn warning. Horns are very underused in the UK, and when they are used, it's usually in an aggressive way to express displeasure at someone else's cackhandedness or mentalism.

The correct use of the horn is as a warning to other road users, so if you see a car and you think the driver hasn't seen you and is about to pull out, give them a quick toot on the horn. It usually gets their attention and stops them pulling out. They may give you one or two fingers (people generally assume you're being aggressive when you use the horn), but at least they will have seen you and you may have prevented them from pulling out. Just give them a cheery wave to take the tension out of the situation and carry on your way.

Be careful with the horn though – it can be counterproductive if you time it badly. If someone does pull out in front of you and you press your horn, a common reaction from the other driver is to hit the brakes and stop – usually half way across the road. So someone pulls out, you brake and swerve to avoid them, expect them to get out of the way and sound your horn and they... stop. Right in front of you. Right in the gap you were expecting to go for.

Sounding the horn too late can, as I said, be counterproductive, so only use it when you think someone is *going* to pull out – not when they *have* done.

Another top tip is summed up in an old advanced driving saying **"where one emerges, another may follow"**. The beard is strong with this saying, but there is a lot of truth in it.

If you see a car pull out of a junction up ahead, there is a strong possibility that it isn't the only one waiting to pull out – there may be one, two, three or a long queue of vehicles behind it, also waiting to pull out.

People behave like sheep sometimes, and when they see the car in front of them emerge and pull out, there is a strong tendency for them to assume it's also safe for them to pull out – after all, the one in front had enough room to go, so there *must* be enough room for me, mustn't there? They're far more likely to make a rash decision based on a very quick (or non-existent) glance, before accelerating out quickly to follow the first car.

So if a vehicle does pull out of a junction ahead of you, think to yourself "it's not that one that's the problem, it's the next one". And if the next one does, in fact, pull out, don't waste time congratulating yourself – think to yourself "and the next one" etc. etc.

If one pulls out, the next one might, and the next one. Remember that one – it's saved me a few times.

It also works particularly well with children on bicycles – they tend to travel around in small packs and if one pulls out, you can almost guarantee that two or three others will follow them.

Disobeyed automatic traffic signal   2%

Let me ask you a question (it's a good one this – try it out on your family and friends!).

What does an amber traffic light mean?

The answers you'll get will be many and varied:

Start to set off.

Get ready to go.

The lights are about to change.

Go.

Proceed with caution.

And any number of other combinations of the above. They're all wrong. An amber light means one thing, and one thing only.

Stop.

If the amber light comes on at the same time as the red light, it means stop. You should not set off until the green light comes on.

If the amber light comes on after the green light, it means stop. You should only continue through the junction if you have already crossed the stop line or if someone is so close behind you that stopping may cause an accident.

So, an amber light means stop.

Why, then, does almost everyone think that you can go through an amber traffic light?

I think it's part of our "rushing everywhere all the time" culture – people desperately feel the need to rush everywhere, to beat the next set of lights, to set off as soon as the amber light comes on – I mean, after all, they've got important places to be and important things to do. Those shoes won't buy themselves will they?

But this "amber gambling" can encourage people to push the limits further and further. Where, a few years ago, it was common to see a few drivers going through lights on amber, it's becoming increasingly common to see drivers going through on red – and not just "as" the red light is coming on, but often one, two, three or more seconds after it has changed. Some push it so far that the opposing lights have changed green when they go through the red light.

You don't need me to explain the substantial risks involved in passing through red lights – they're there for a very obvious reason and no-one should be passing through an amber light, let alone a red one.

So you should go back to the start of this section & re-read what an amber light means. Start putting it into practice – don't set off till the green light is on and if the light goes from green to amber, stop. If you follow this fairly straightforward advice, you'll avoid points and carnage!

Other Drivers

But – as with many other sections of this book – it's not just you is it? As I've already mentioned, there are loads of people out there gambling with our lives and no-claims-bonuses by dashing through red traffic lights when they shouldn't. How do you avoid them?

The answer, yet again, is to use your imagination. Many drivers wait at red traffic lights staring intently at the lights, willing them to change. Others, when stopped at lights, take the opportunity to check their phone, update their Facebook status, check their hair and makeup in the mirror, bollock the children and look in shop windows. When the lights change to green, they assume it's safe to go and set off, without a care in the world. It's a green light, after all.

But if you keep your wits about you, spend your time when stationary looking around you, looking at how traffic is behaving in the rest of the junction, and checking the opposing lights, you'll be far more likely to spot the occasional driver who is willing to risk running a red light. You may be stationary when you're waiting at a traffic light, but you're still *driving*, so you should still *think* like a driver. Look around you, use your imagination and think about what *might* happen. If you do this, occasionally the "might" will turn into "will" and you'll save yourself some pain and grief.

In busy cities – London is particularly bad at the moment – there are many cyclists who treat traffic lights with a level of disdain. You'd think, wouldn't you, that as one of the most vulnerable road users, cyclists would be extra careful at traffic lights? There are, however, a substantial minority of cyclists who will happily dive through lights which have been red for some time, and then weave in and out of the opposing traffic. Sometimes accompanied by shouting and swearing and a generally bad attitude.

These cyclists are another reason that you should stay aware and keep looking round you even when you're stationary at traffic lights.

There are one set of road users who regularly go through red traffic lights because they are legally exempt from stopping at red lights – emergency service drivers.

When they're on an emergency "blues and twos" run, emergency services drivers are taught to treat red traffic lights as a "give way" junction, so they should slow right down and cross through red lights at quite a slow speed, allowing everyone enough time to react to their actions.

There are, however, occasions when emergency drivers don't give traffic lights sufficient caution – police officers may be on their way to a call for urgent assistance from a colleague, for instance, or pursuing a stolen car. Firefighters may be on their way to a fire "persons reported" which could be a life-and-death call. These drivers are always taught to ignore the severity of the call and to drive to the same standard, irrespective of the nature of the incident.

They're only human though, and if they think a colleague's life is in danger or that people are dying in a fire, there is a possibility (right or wrong – I'm not judging) that they may ignore their training and take more risks on route to the incident – including risking the odd red light junction at speed.

It's called "noble cause risk taking" and it's something you should be aware of. It doesn't happen very often, but it's important when you're approaching a traffic light junction (whether the lights are in your favour or not), that you keep an eye – and an ear – out for approaching emergency services vehicles.

Keeping an ear out is particularly important. If you drive with your music turned up to 11, there is a strong possibility that you won't hear approaching sirens, so keep your music levels reasonable and listen out for the woo-woo's!

Another issue to be aware of if you live or travel in a busy city, is that it's very easy to become "siren immune". If you spend any time in a busy city, you'll know that there is very little time when you *can't* hear the whooping and wailing of a siren somewhere. It's an almost constant background noise in many large cities, to the point that people pay very little attention to sirens.

Try to not let yourself become immune – if you hear a siren, look around you – to the sides and in your mirrors. If you're at a junction, look out for the lights. They'll be there somewhere!

Cyclist entering road from pavement   1%

1% (917) of accidents are caused by cyclists entering the road from the pavement.

I know that people should take responsibility for their own actions, and that cyclists, as vulnerable road users, should be particularly aware of their own vulnerability and take extra care when entering a road from a pavement, and most do, but...

Some don't – and I'm sure you've seen many cyclists emerge suddenly into the road without looking or signalling and seemingly without any warning at all.

But, there are some clues which cyclists give off – often without even realising it themselves – that they are about to pull onto the road, and if you can learn to spot these clues, you may avoid being involved in one of these types of accidents.

Firstly, train yourself to look just as carefully at what's happening on the pavements as you do at what's happening on the road itself. Be aware of the movements of everyone on the pavements and look carefully for the ones who may cause you a problem.

In particular, if you spot a cyclist on the pavement, you should always have in the back of your mind, the possibility that they may enter the road without looking. Look for people getting onto bicycles, scooting along slowly on a bicycle, or weaving around pedestrians on the pavement.

Cyclists often give their intentions away with their head movements. A quick glance over their right shoulder often means they're about to turn right – or in the case of a cyclist on the pavement, it often means they're about to join the road, so if you see a cyclist on the pavement give a quick look backwards, be ready for them to emerge onto the road in front of you.

Children on bicycles can be particularly unpredictable and have a tendency to emerge quickly from driveways and entrances in urban and suburban areas. Keep your observations wide and look to the sides as well as in front when you're driving in these areas. If a child does emerge suddenly in front of you, remember what I said earlier about them travelling in packs, and look for the others – it's not the one which pulls out that the problem – it's the next one, and the next one!

If you see a cyclist on the pavement, move away from them – towards the centre of the road, so that if they do pull out in front of you, you've got a zone of relative safety around your car and there is less chance that you'll hit them. Effectively, you should treat a cyclist on the pavement in exactly the same way as you would treat them if they were on the road – give them as much space as you would if you were passing them on the road.

Illegal turn or direction of travel   1%

This accounts for 1% of all accidents (703 accidents) and refers specifically to drivers who drive the wrong way into one-way systems or the wrong way along motorways or dual carriageways.

I've given this some considerable thought, and my best advice on this factor is not to drive the wrong way down one-way streets or onto motorways!

These incidents are thankfully quite rare, but I struggle to comprehend sometimes how anyone can get things so wrong that they manage to completely circumvent all the road markings, junction designs and signs which are designed to prevent people driving the wrong way onto motorways, and then fail to stop when they're suddenly faced by thousands of terrified motorists coming the other way! I mean – it must be obvious to them mustn't it?

So, I'll assume you're not daft enough to drive the wrong way along the motorway, but what should you do if someone else is? These incidents are rare, but what should you do if you see someone coming towards you on the motorway?

My best advice is to sit in the middle lane and slow down. Most of these types of drivers have either accidentally driven on to the wrong carriageway, or are trying to evade the police, so they'll either drive on the hard shoulder or in the outside (2nd, 3rd or 4th lane, depending on the width of the motorway). With that in mind, your best course of action is to slow and drive in the middle lane – usually lane 2, or lane 1 on a two-lane motorway.

Disobeyed pedestrian crossing facility 0% (540)

This contributory factor accounts for 507 accidents per year in the UK – a small number, but still 507 accidents which could have easily been avoided if people just looked out for each other a bit more. Most of these accidents involved pedestrians too, so the likelihood of casing a death or serious injury by disobeying a pedestrian crossing is much higher.

I thought the best way to address this issue is to take a quick look at all the different types of pedestrian crossings in the UK – some of which you'll be familiar with and some of which you'll be less familiar with. Let's start with...

Zebra Crossings

Zebra crossings are the oldest type of pedestrian crossing still in use in the UK. They consist of a black and white striped area on the road surface (hence "zebra"), black and white-striped poles on the pavement at each side of the crossing, topped with round flashing yellow lights (Belisha beacons), and zig-zag markings on the road either side of the crossing.

You MUST give way to anyone who has started to cross the road at a zebra crossing.

There is no legal requirement for you to stop for anyone waiting at a zebra crossing, but it's common courtesy and unless doing so might cause an accident (if someone is very close behind you, for example), you should always stop if you see someone waiting to cross.

One thing you mustn't do, however, is wave pedestrians across. By all means stop, but you should wait and let them make their own mind up whether it's safe to cross or not. It might feel like you're helping people out, but, in fact, other vehicles may not have stopped, or seen what is happening, and waving people across may put them in danger of an accident, so just stop and keep your hands on the wheel.

When the crossing is clear and you're about to set off again, it's always worth having a quick check left and right to make sure no-one else intends to cross – some people may make a last-minute dash for the crossing and you need to have a look for them before you set off, so mirror and shoulder checks are really important when you're moving off from a zebra crossing.

School Crossings

School crossings are "manned" crossing points which operate outside schools before and after the school day (and sometimes at lunchtimes).

School crossing patrolmen and patrolwomen are employed by the local authority to help children and their parents to cross the road to and from school. They are equipped with high-visibility clothing and a large "Stop" sign mounted on a long black and white pole.

We're all familiar with "lollipop men" and "lollipop women" aren't we? But there's a couple of things you might not know about them.

Their "lollipop" sign has a thick black horizontal bar across the middle. When school crossing patrols were first introduced in 1967, along with their sign, they were issued with a piece of chalk, so that they could write down the registration numbers of cars which had failed to stop, on the black horizontal bar.

Their sign can be used in a number of ways. If the lollipop person holds the sign upside down, with the sign part touching the ground, it means they're not ready to cross pedestrians & you can drive past them with caution.

It can also be held horizontally as a barrier to stop children from crossing until it is safe to do so.

When the lollipop person is ready to stop the traffic, they will stand on the pavement and hold their sign out high, angled out towards the traffic. If you see this signal, you should prepare to stop for the crossing.

When traffic does stop, the lollipop person will step into the road and stand in the centre with the "stop" sign held vertically to their side so that traffic from both directions can see it.

It is an offence to fail to stop for a school crossing patrol, and bearing in mind the additional hazards present around schools at peak times, there can never be an excuse for failing to see, or stop for a lollipop person.

In the past, school crossing patrols were only allowed to stop traffic to allow children to cross, but a change to the law in 2000 means that they are now authorised to stop traffic to allow anyone to cross the road (not that this should matter to you! Why would you *not* stop for a lollipop person?!)

It is becoming increasingly common to see school crossing patrols on duty alongside an additional crossing, such as a pelican crossing. This gives children an additional safety measure and there is one important thing that you should bear in mind. When the lollipop man or woman is on duty, their sign takes precedence over the fixed crossing.

So, if the lights on a pelican crossing turn back to green whilst the lollipop person still has their sign displayed, you cannot move off until they have cleared the crossing. Even if the crossing remains on green throughout, if the crossing patrol steps out with their sign, you *must* stop.

Pelican Crossings

Pelican Crossings are "Signal Control" crossings – crossings which use traffic lights controlled by the pedestrians waiting to cross. "Pelican" stands for "**PE**desrian **LI**ght **Co**Ntrolled crossing". Not sure what happened with the "a", but there you go.

Pelican crossings are marked with traffic lights on both sides of the road (and sometimes also in the middle if there is a reservation) and zig-zag lines on the road either side of the crossing. They also often have barriers or fences to prevent people from entering the road away from the crossing.

If you're approaching a pelican crossing, have a look to see if there is anyone waiting at the crossing – this could mean that the lights are about to change from green to amber and red and that you'll have to stop.

If you do have to stop, the traffic lights have a slightly different phasing. Instead of going red - red & amber – green, the red light is followed by a flashing amber phase. If the red light changes to flashing amber, you MUST give way to anyone already on the crossing. If the crossing is clear, you are allowed to set off carefully.

But as we're all keen on looking after each other, it's important to remember that you should give way to any pedestrians in the road, even if the lights are on green.

Don't forget – before you set off, remember to have a good look all around you to make sure no-one is going to cross at the last minute.

Puffin Crossings

Puffin crossings are signal – or traffic light – controlled crossings. "Puffin" stands for "**P**edestrian **U**ser **F**riendly **IN**telligent crossing". They are similar to pelican crossings in that they are marked with traffic lights and zig-zag lines, but they do differ in two main ways.

Firstly, these crossings are fitted with sensors which detect whether pedestrians are still in the road and keep the traffic lights on red whilst they are still crossing.

Secondly, there is no flashing amber phase on the traffic lights – once the sensors confirm that the crossing is clear, the lights change to red & amber and then green in the normal way.

That's all well and good and these crossings seem to keep traffic flowing a little better whilst making it safer for pedestrians, but the same caution should be used when you're approaching and negotiating puffin crossings. On the approach, look for people waiting at the crossing & expect the lights to change if you do. And be very careful when you set off again because there is still the risk that someone will try to cross at the last minute as the lights are changing.

Toucan Crossings

Toucan Crossings are very similar to puffin crossings, but they allow cyclists to cross as well as pedestrians (Two-Can Cross).

They look very similar to puffin and pelican crossings, but some do not have the usual zig-zag markings. The advice for pelican and puffin crossings is also relevant to toucan crossings, but with the additional warning that cyclists may also make that last-minute dive for the crossing just as you're about to set off. To make this more of a risk, they are likely to be travelling faster than pedestrians when they do, so you should look even more carefully behind and all around you before setting off after stopping at one of these crossings.

Pegasus Crossings

Pegasus crossings are very similar to Toucan and Puffin crossings, but with an additional high-level button for horse riders. You'll normally find these types of crossings in areas where there is a lot of equestrian activity, such as large stables, racetracks etc.

At the risk of repeating myself again, look for the same things you would with the other type of pedestrian crossings & give horses plenty of time to clear the road before you set off, as there aren't many things that are more dangerous than a ton of startled horse!

A Couple of Other Points

Firstly, the zig-zag lines are present at pedestrian crossings for a very good reason – they keep the immediate vicinity of the crossing clear, allowing pedestrians to have a good view in both directions and, crucially, to allow you to have a good view of the pedestrians as you approach a crossing. It's really important then, that you don't contravene these markings by parking on them – even for a short time. It's an endorsable offence, meaning you could get points on your licence, and you could contribute towards an accident.

Secondly, if you're travelling in heavy stop-start traffic and you encounter a pedestrian crossing, you should try to keep the crossing itself clear by not stopping in the middle. The crossing is defined by some distinctive square metal studs and you should wait until there is enough room on the other side of the crossing for your car to clear the metal studs before you move forward.

Vehicle Travelling Along Pavement   0% (273)

263 accidents were caused by vehicles travelling along the pavement, which is only a tiny percentage of accidents per year, but also included 9 fatal accidents, which is more significant.

There isn't really a lot of advice I can give you in relation to this contributory factor other than advising you not to drive on the pavement.

So don't drive on the pavement!

Having said that, it is becoming more and more commonplace for people to park their cars half-on and half-off the pavement these days and one thing I'm seeing more and more frequently is drivers parking on the pavement by driving up a dropped kerb some distance from where they intend to park and continuing – sometimes at a reasonable speed – to drive along the pavement until they've reached their planned parking spot.

This presents a number of risks, not least of which is the risk that someone will walk out of their house and drive to be met with a car travelling at speed along the pavement.

If you intend to park on the pavement, stay on the road until you're very close to your parking spot before mounting the kerb. If you're bothered about scuffing your wheels, don't do it at a shallow angle – instead, turn your wheels so that they are almost on full lock and mount the pavement slowly – that way you'll keep the edges of your wheels away from the kerb and the face of your tyre will take the wheel up the kerb without damage.

Disobeyed Double White Lines   0% (214)

209 accidents were caused by someone disobeying double white lines, but 21 of those accidents were fatal, so we should look at double-white lines, what they mean and why they are used.

Double white lines are positioned in the centre of the road on corners and other areas of road where it would be dangerous for vehicles to cross into the opposing carriageway or lane. There are two types of double white line:

Double solid white lines – these mean the same irrespective of what direction you may be travelling in – you must not cross, straddle or park alongside double solid white lines.

Double white lines where one line is broken – if the line nearest to you is solid, as with double solid lines, you must not cross, straddle or park alongside the line. If the line nearest to you is broken, you can cross or straddle the line if it's safe to do so, but you still must not park alongside the broken line.

There are some exemptions, so if you encounter a stationary vehicle or a cyclist, horse or works vehicle travelling at less that 10mph, you're allowed to cross the white lines to pass them if it's safe.

You'll find these markings in a few different areas, but the most common is on single-carriageway roads with blind, or limited-view corners. These are corners where, without double-white lines, you may be tempted to take a bit of a "racing" line by cutting and straightening the corner. The placement of double white lines discourages people from cutting corners where they may come into conflict with oncoming vehicles.

In my experience, these road markings tend only to be used where they are really needed, so it's important that you take their guidance and stay to the left of any solid white lines you encounter. The road designers even help you by warning that you're about to encounter double-whites. They paint white "direction" arrows on the road on the lead-up to double white lines to give you the opportunity to return to the nearside if you need to. They are a large arrow with a slight curve to the left & if you look for them, you'll see them much more frequently than you might expect.

You'll also see double white lines at, and on the approach to a number of different junctions, roundabouts etc., and you'll also see them on single carriageway roads with more than one lane in each direction.

Parking alongside these lines is a bad idea, as you'll be forcing traffic to cross the lines right at the point that the road engineers have identified that it's dangerous to cross them, so please don't!

One thing many people don't seem to be aware of is that it's an offence to park alongside double white lines *even if the line nearest to you is broken*. People seem to think that, as it's ok to cross the broken white line, it's ok to park alongside it, but it isn't & you could receive an endorsable fixed penalty (3 penalty points) just for parking next to double-white lines, whether they are broken on your side or not.

4. ROAD ENVIRONMENT CONTRIBUTED (13% OF ALL ACCIDENTS)

Our roads are in pretty poor condition at the moment. It's down to a combination of lack of long-term investment in the road infrastructure and the massive increase in traffic over the last 25 years.

Poor road surfaces can cause a variety of different problems for drivers, so it's worth looking at each of the individual factors in turn & sharing my best advice for dealing with these issues and avoiding letting them become accidents.

Slippery road (due to weather)   8%

Let's start with the most common road surface issue we encounter in the UK:

Wet or damp roads

A wet road surface has less grip, but on the road, the difference isn't as much as you might think, as long as you're sensible and always drive within your, and the car's abilities.

Tyre condition is very important on a damp or wet road surface – it is the tyre's tread which removes water and allows the tyre to grip with the road surface, and as we all know, tyre grip is all important and can drastically affect your ability to accelerate, brake and corner – all the activities of driving, in fact. So make sure your tyres are in good condition and the pressures are correct.

Look out for standing water. If you keep an eye on the design of the road surface i.e. how it is designed to drain, you'll get a clue as to where the standing water will be.

On a traditional "crown camber" road, the centre of the road is higher than the nearside and offside kerbs, so the water will drain to both sides and you can expect puddles to form on both sides of the road. If the road is crown camber and the water has spread across the entire width of the road, then your best position, if there is no oncoming traffic, is right in the centre of the road, straddling the white line, as this is will be where the water is shallowest.

On a more modern road which is built with "super elevation", the corners will be consistently banked with the inside of the corner at the lowest point and the outside of the bend being the highest point. In simple terms, this means that on super elevated roads, whichever direction you are travelling in, water will build up on the inside of corners. Be ready to adjust your position away from the inside and be ready to adjust your position to allow opposing drivers to do the same.

As for standing water, it can cause aquaplaning if driven through inappropriately. Aquaplaning occurs when a "wedge" of water builds up between the front of the tyre and the road surface and the tyre tread can no longer effectively disperse all the water from under the tyre. In even simpler terms, the car effectively starts to "float" across the water and you can no longer steer, brake or accelerate. Not good.

To avoid the worst effects of aquaplaning, if you spot some standing water ahead, try to roll through it without making any driving inputs whatsoever. Lift off the throttle, don't brake, don't steer and roll through in a straight line. Grip will resume once you are out of the water.

Hitting standing water with the wheels on one side of the car can cause a dramatic "pull" towards that side of the car. So if you hit a puddle on the nearside at speed, the car will pull hard to the left. Try to drive round puddles when you can, and keep your speed down & increase your grip on the steering wheel if you can't. Don't forget that puddles can hide potholes, so it's never a good idea to plough through them at unreduced speed if you value your expensive alloy wheels.

If the road appears to be flooded, do not risk driving through unless you're absolutely sure of the depth of the water and the position of your car's air intake. If you spot a flood, turn around and go the other way. You really don't want to be one of those people in one of those pictures published by one of those newspapers. Even if it's a 30-mile detour, take it!

During autumn, wet roads are made more slippery by the helpful addition of wet leaves and leaf mulch. This can be very slippery – look out for it and adjust your speed accordingly.

Frost

If you get up in the morning and you have to scrape ice off your windscreen, then there is a very good chance there will be ice on the road. This might sound ridiculously obvious, but you would not believe how many people don't make this very simple observation link and after defrosting their car, go out and drive just as if it's a bright sunny day.

I've been informed by people with meteroeoloeoloeologiclogical (!) knowledge that the temperature gauges fitted to cars are not very accurate, but in my view they do at least give an indication when the temperature is getting close to freezing. Mine gives off an ominous "bong" when it drops below 3 degrees and flashes up a warning on the dashboard. This can be helpful when you're driving from day into night or from low to high altitude, as in those circumstances, it's not usually obvious to a driver in a nice warm car, that the temperature is dropping outside.

Frost forms a slightly grey-coloured coating on untreated roads, and it's not easy to spot, particularly at night. The good thing is that, actually, it isn't as slippery as you might think and it's quite possible to drive normally on a frosty road surface as long as you are aware that there is a little less grip, that you need a little more time to stop and a little less speed when cornering.

Keep all your inputs smooth and consistent. Be careful in how you transfer the car's weight around when operating the controls & try to "taper" your inputs. Avoid clumsy, clumpy and clonky inputs as these are more likely to result in a loss of control when Jack Frost is out.

Sheet / Black ice

This is significantly different to frost. Sheet or "black" ice is actually frozen puddles or frozen standing water on the road surface. It is as slippery as – well – as slippery as ice and can be absolutely treacherous if you're not careful.

Keep in mind all the awareness stuff I spoke about in the last section and the stuff I spoke about relating to standing water & where it forms in the first section. Black ice is frozen standing water - it looks just like standing water and it forms in exactly the same areas that standing water forms.

If you unexpectedly drive onto sheet ice, the first thing you'll notice is an almost complete lack of any tyre noise whatsoever – silence suddenly descends in the vehicle cabin.

There will be virtually no grip whatsoever between the tyres and the road surface, so avoid making any inputs whilst driving over black ice. If you turn the wheel, the car will keep going in a straight line until you leave the ice – at which point you will regain grip, and the car will suddenly shoot off in the direction you have pointed the wheel, which can lead to a sudden loss of control.

So, if you're caught out by black ice, slide over it and then make any necessary corrections *after* regaining grip with the road surface. If you're on an ocean of sheet ice and heading for an accident, muller your brakes and keep them fully on. ABS will help you make the most of the tiny amount of grip available and if nothing else, will reduce the speed of the impact.

Snow is the weather condition which seems to create more problems than anything else in this country due to people's general inability to slightly alter their driving style to suit.

I'm not going into much detail about snow tyres & 4-wheel drive, other than to say that winter tyres can make a huge difference in any winter weather conditions and 4-wheel drive can improve your traction on a slippery road (although not as much as many people think), but gives no advantage in braking or steering.

If there is very heavy and consistent snow which is settling on the road surface, then snow chains, socks etc. will help with traction, but they must be fitted to the driven wheels.

In light snow, you should adopt a smooth, steady driving style in much the same way as I described earlier in relation to a frosty road surface.

One mistake many people make is to assume that you must drive very slowly in snow. In fact, it's important to maintain reasonable momentum, because traction is the issue – particularly on uphill stretches. If you crawl up a hill you're very likely to run out of traction and get stuck, whereas if you maintain some momentum and keep going, you're far more likely to make it up the hill.

In deep snow, there is an advantage in turning off your traction control to allow a little wheel-spin. I don't mean you should sit there with your wheels lit up, but a little slip can help to increase traction, particularly when moving off from stationary.

Tyre tracks form very quickly in snow, and at anything above 20-25 mph, moving out of these tracks onto the undisturbed snow can seriously unsettle the car. This is particularly noticeable on dual carriageways and motorways. Unless it's absolutely necessary, try to avoid changing lanes, and if you have to, do it very gradually with minimal, smooth inputs.

On exposed roads, snow can drift onto the road from adjacent fields. Look for gaps in hedges and fences, as this is where the snow will drift.

Hail

A hailstorm can be very unpredictable and can occur at any time of the year. It is most dangerous when it falls on a cold day on a dry road, and can be similar to driving on to millions of tiny ball bearings or marbles.

If you encounter sudden hail, just be aware of the immediate reduction in road grip and drive accordingly.

Road layout (e.g. bend, hill, narrow road)   3%

I struggle with this one a bit – if a driver fails to appreciate the road layout, and has an accident as a result, how can the road layout be a contributory factor? The road isn't to blame – it's the driver who's got things wrong.

On the other hand, some road features can be more hazardous than others and require an element of greater care on the part of the driver.

Suffice to say, I think there is more than enough information on all of these issues in the rest of this book, so I'd only be repeating myself if I started going into detail here. The only thing I will repeat is the safe stopping rule, which should help you with any issues to do with unsafe road layouts:

You should always be able to stop, on your own side of the road, in the distance you can see to be clear.

Keep this in mind, and no amount of poor road layouts should catch you out.

When cornering, in extremely basic terms, you should approach a corner in the correct position (to the nearside for a right-hand corner and to the offside for a left-hand corner), get your speed and gear correct *before* you get to the corner, and then steer and accelerate gently through the corner.

If you want to learn more about cornering and how to assess corners properly, I've covered the subject in much detail in my book "Advanced & Performance Driving".

Deposit on road (e.g. oil, mud, chippings)   1%

The first key skill to master with this contributory factor is spotting the deposits on the road before you drive onto them. Some are easier to spot than others, but there are additional clues you can use to help you to anticipate the areas and times when you're more likely to encounter deposits on the road surface.

Mud, chippings, soil etc. are reasonably easy to spot if you're looking in the right places and considering the road surface as part of your driving plans.

In rural areas, farmers often trail mud and debris in and out of farmyards and field entrances. If you see a farm in the distance, you should always make the mental link with the possibility that there will be mud and detritus spread across the road.

Where you see trails of mud leading out of a field, there is also the possibility that you'll encounter the tractor travelling slowly a little further along the road, so you should also keep that possibility within your driving plans.

Building sites, construction projects, roadworks and quarries also bring with them the likelihood that mud, chippings and other muck may be spread across the road by vehicles leaving the site, so always make the mental link when you see these types of areas and be prepared to deal with a dirty road surface.

Fuel, oil etc. is much more difficult to spot. On a wet road, oil, petrol and diesel leaves a "rainbow" like sheen on the surface of puddles and wet roads. On a dry road, it's even more difficult to spot – the best clue is that tyre marks made by other vehicles through a puddle of water will end very quickly, whereas those left by vehicles which have driven through a fuel or oil puddle will last much longer on a dry road.

Your sense of smell comes into play as well – ask any motorcyclist how their senses go onto full alert if they smell diesel whilst they're riding along. If you get a smell of diesel or kerosene, there may well be a fuel spillage on the road surface.

When you're driving over a slippery road surface, keep your speed down and your inputs smooth and controlled. Avoid any sudden or jerky steering or braking and if you do need to brake or accelerate, you should do it gently and progressively.

Be aware that – no matter how good you are at spotting and dealing with slippery road surfaces – other drivers may not be as good, so look out for the other idiots and be prepared to avoid them!

Animal or object in carriageway   1%

Animals can be extremely unpredictable and an animal running into the carriageway can be very hazardous. They can also cause a considerable amount of damage – I've seen cars heavily damaged after hitting a dog or badger and totally written off after hitting a small deer.

If you continue to work on improving your observation skills, you'll continue to get better at spotting animals early – or even before they run into the road. You should also be able to pick up the visual clues that animals may be around.

Firstly, when you see someone walking their dog, always look to see if the dog is on a lead and under control. If it's not, you should slow and give the dog a wide birth – even well trained dogs can act unpredictably and against the wishes of their owners sometimes. Even if the dog is on a lead, you should be aware that it may suddenly jump into the road, and give it as much space as is safe.

There are areas of road where you're more likely to encounter wild or domesticated animals in the road. If you're in a rural area, you should always associate farms and field entrances with the possibility that there may be animals in the road – a rabbit or pheasant at best - a herd of cattle being moved by the farmer at worst. Drive so that you can stop in the distance you can see to be clear.

If an animal does run out unexpectedly in front of you, your natural reaction will be to brake and try to avoid hitting the animal. This is normal and I'm not in any way trying to discourage you from doing the same.

However, many people fail to take into account the fact that there may be other hazards around at the time – oncoming vehicles, for instance, or pedestrians on the footpath. My advice is that if swerving to avoid an animal could cause a more serious accident, then you shouldn't swerve. If it's a choice between hitting a cat or hitting an oncoming lorry, you should hit the cat.

Don't get me wrong – hitting a cat or other animal is very unpleasant, but sometimes you need to very quickly weigh the risks up in your mind and, occasionally, hitting the animal rather than the other stuff is the right thing to do.

Objects

The phrase "objects in the carriageway" mostly refers to unexpected foreign objects which have become detached from a vehicle whilst travelling along a motorway or dual carriageway. During my policing career I retrieved hundreds of objects from motorways, from ladders and buckets through to dead dogs and tailor's dummies!

When you're travelling at speed on the motorway, you can "arrive" at these objects extremely quickly and because there are often vehicles to your left and right, your only option is to hit them and take whatever damage occurs. Only last week I was faced with this dilemma and I chose to hit the debris rather than swerve into the vehicles which were alongside me. Fortunately, it was just a small piece of plasterboard which had fallen from a builder's van, so there was no damage, but I'm sure you can see the dangers involved.

Firstly – try to spot these items as early as possible. It isn't easy – I proved that last week – but if you look well ahead, you can sometimes see debris much further down the road, and make an early move to avoid it.

Look ahead for tell-tale signs from other cars – look for sudden braking and swerving for no apparent reason – they could be trying to avoid an object in the carriageway.

If the worst comes to the worst (like it did for me last week), remember that you're travelling at speed and any sudden steering inputs could lead to a loss of control. Steer round the object if at all possible, but if you've got other vehicles to the left and/or right of you, there may be no other safe option other than to hit the object.

If you do, you should stop on the hard shoulder as soon as it's safe to do so and check your car for damage. You should also ring 999 and report the debris before it causes any further accidents.

Poor or defective road surface   1% (793)

Slippery inspection cover or road marking   0% (44)

As I mentioned earlier in this chapter, our roads are in a pretty poor state at the moment, with pot-holes and pock-marks on almost every road in the UK.

Modern tyres and suspension are pretty durable and will cope with most pot-holes and other road defects, but it's important, wherever possible, to avoid the very worst pot-holes as they can damage your tyres and wheels and – at worst – lead to a loss of control and an accident.

When you're driving – along with all the other stuff you're looking at, you should regularly check the road surface for defects. The earlier you spot them the earlier you'll be able to avoid them, by driving around them or straddling them.

If you're driving in traffic, keep a nice, long following distance from the vehicle in front – as well as the other advantages I've detailed elsewhere in this book, a good following distance will also allow you to spot any serious road defects with enough time to avoid them.

If avoiding a pothole means that you'll have to drive into the opposing carriageway, make sure it's clear before you do – it's no good hitting an oncoming car just to avoid a pothole!

"Inspection covers" are really manhole covers and because they're generally made from metal or plastic, they can be much more slippery than the surrounding road surface – particularly when they're wet.

Tram lines are particularly bad – if you live in an area where trams run alongside normal traffic, you should always avoid driving on the rails themselves as they're very slippery. Instead, always make sure your tyres are straddling the tram lines and running along the road surface, rather than the tram lines themselves.

Inadequate or masked signs or road markings

0% (461)

As our roads have deteriorated, so have the standards of road signs and road markings & it's becoming increasingly common to see road signs badly obscured by hedges and trees, and road markings which have virtually worn away completely.

If you're sensible and intelligent in your driving, however, there is no reason whatsoever that poor road signs or markings should cause you to have an accident.

Signs and markings are only there to *help* you work out what hazards are ahead and how to negotiate them. You shouldn't rely on them entirely to tell you what to do and what to expect – instead you should learn to read the *whole* road by looking at the entire environment and working out what's coming and what you should do about it.

Temporary road layout (e.g. contraflow) 0% (276)

A contraflow system is a roadworks system designed to allow work to be carried out on some or all of an entire carriageway by diverting traffic onto the opposite carriageway **contra**ry to the normal **flow** of traffic. The danger is that, rather than being separated from opposing traffic by a central reservation and Armco barriers, traffic is generally only separated by a line of those skinny traffic cones, or, at best, a temporary concrete barrier.

An ex police driving school colleague of mine had worked as a motorway patrol officer for many years, and he had seen one too many crossover accidents in contraflow systems. He wouldn't allow his students to use the right-hand lane in any contraflow system on the basis that, even in a reduced speed limit area, the risks of a head-on collision due to a simple lane change error were too great.

I take a slightly more flexible approach, whereby as long as there is some clear space to my left; I'm comfortable using the right-most lane. In other words, try not to linger alongside other vehicles. If the speed of traffic is similar in both lanes, then try to make sure you're alongside a gap rather than a vehicle. And of course, the leftmost lane *is* the safest option if you're not too bothered about progress, which is usually severely hampered by temporary speed limits anyway.

Defective traffic signals   0% (135)

When traffic lights are out, the main thing to bear in mind is that *no-one* has priority over anyone else. In other words, you should assume that no-one will stop, bring your speed right down to a crawl, and gently progress through the junction, watching each and every other vehicle for clues as to whether they're yielding, or going.

This may sound really dangerous and complicated, but whenever I've encountered broken traffic lights at a busy junction, the traffic actually seems to flow a lot better than when the lights are working.

Just take your time, take your cue from the other drivers and be cautious and you'll be fine.

Traffic calming (e.g. road humps, chicane) 0% (131)

This is a very small number of accidents and recognises the fact that some drivers drive inappropriately quickly over traffic calming measures.

"Traffic calming measures" include speed bumps, speed cushions, sleeping policemen, chicanes and narrow "pinch points", and you'll generally find them installed on roads where there are a large number of hazards and where other efforts to reduce the speed of traffic have failed.

The thing to bear in mind here is that your speed should already be low enough for you to negotiate these roads safely with a minimum of risk. If you're daft enough to drive inappropriately fast on these roads *and* lose control because of the traffic calming measures which have been installed in an effort to *prevent* you from driving too fast, then, I'm afraid, there's no hope for you!

5. IMPAIRMENT OR DISTRACTION (13% OF ALL ACCIDENTS)

Driver/Rider impaired by alcohol   4%

When I started the initial research for this book, this figure really surprised me – drink driving is portrayed as a major cause of serious and fatal accidents in the UK and we've all been subject to a great deal of anti-drink-drive publicity over the years, yet only 4% of all accidents are attributed by the reporting officer as being caused, in part, by a driver who was impaired by alcohol.

If we put that figure into context, however, and examine the statistics in more detail, you'll see that drink driving is still a serious problem in the UK.

4% equates to 4,679 accidents, 1,034 of which resulted in someone being seriously injured and 128 of which resulted in someone being killed. 128 is actually 9% of all fatal accidents which occur in the UK, so if we were only examining fatalities, excess alcohol contributes to a large percentage of road deaths.

128 people killed in 12 months. Imagine the furore if 128 people were killed every year on the railways. There would be a public enquiry, many millions would be spent on improving rail safety, lines and trains would be redesigned and people would think twice about travelling by train.

But because these deaths are occurring on the road, we quietly accept them, momentarily feel sorry for the bereaved families when we read about these accidents in the paper, and then turn the page to read the football results.

Why is alcohol such a problem?

Let's start by looking at what alcohol is, what effects it has on your body, and why these effects are so incompatible with driving a motor vehicle:

Alcohol is a depressant

This may come as a bit of a surprise, especially if you associate alcohol with partying, dancing and raving the night away, but alcohol is, chemically and physiologically, a depressant. By "depressant", I don't mean that it makes you want to listen to The Smiths and cry at the end of Titanic – I mean that in chemical terms, it depresses a number of functions of your brain and nervous system. Let's look at how it affects you from your first drink onwards and see how compatible those effects are with driving a motor vehicle.

First Drink:

Alcohol is absorbed very quickly by your body and will start to affect you almost immediately after taking your first drink. The first effects are that the parts of your brain which control inhibitions, concentration, willpower and self-control are depressed by the alcohol.

Socially, these effects are generally considered to be good and they're the reason that many of us enjoy a drink from time-to-time. With lowered inhibitions and increased self-confidence, we tend to talk more and louder and behave in a more socially outgoing, extrovert and unreserved way.

That first drink or two also starts to affect your "fine motor skills" – your ability to control your hands and fingers to carry out detailed tasks. It also affects your peripheral vision in an interesting way – the background and areas to each side become blurred and you become less able to focus on what is happening around you and more focussed on what is just immediately in front of you.

Compatibility with Driving

These effects can clearly be pleasant, particularly in a social setting, but how compatible are they with driving a car? The problems are threefold:

Firstly, your increased self-confidence will make you *think* that you're a better driver than you are and that you'll actually be *better* at driving a car than you would be when you're completely sober.

Secondly, your depressed visual acuity and motor skills will generally reduce your ability to operate a cars controls and properly assess what you're seeing.

Thirdly, your lowered inhibitions will make you less likely to refuse to drive, and more likely to confidently get in your car and encourage other people to join you.

These effects can occur after consumption of quite small quantities of alcohol – sometimes well below legal drink-drive limits, so it's important to remember that even if you're legally allowed to drive after one drink, it will still have these effects on your body and you will still be impaired to a degree.

As You Continue Drinking

As your consumption of alcohol increases, the effects on your body and cognitive functions become more pronounced. By the time you're on your third or fourth drink, you'll generally start to slur your words (even though you may not notice the slurring), and your peripheral and background vision will be much more blurred and insignificant.

Your fine motor skills will deteriorate to a much greater degree (you'll feel quite clumsy and may knock things over or drop things you'd never normally drop), your balance is starting to be affected and your ability to make sensible, rational decisions reduces significantly.

Compatibility with Driving

At this point, you're starting to feel a bit drunk – tipsy, merry, squiffy, giddy – the level of drunkenness where you can still function reasonably. You know what you're doing and where you are, but you're also very relaxed, even more outgoing, your voice is even more raised and you're starting to become a little unsteady on your feet.

Unfortunately, those earlier feelings of confidence and lowered inhibitions are still with you – possibly to an even greater degree, so you're still – at this point – more likely to think your driving will be fine and to make the decision that it'll be ok to drive.

Clearly, though, it won't be. These more significant effects of alcohol are not compatible with keeping safe control of a vehicle. Your ability to take in visual and other information is reduced, your ability to process that information quickly and accurately drops significantly and your ability to make rational decisions and plans is diminished.

In addition, your ability to control your hand and foot movements, together with your balance and hand-eye co-ordination are also significantly reduced, meaning that your ability to operate the cars controls are considerably depleted.

In short, you can't see or think properly and you can't operate the cars controls as well as when you're sober.

This level of drunkenness generally falls above the legal drink-drive limits and if you've drunk enough alcohol to reach this level or worse, then you pose a significant risk if you get behind the wheel (or handlebars, tiller, yolk, control column, whatever your choice of mechanised transport).

More Please!

Beyond this stage, the effects on your body and brain become much more pronounced. Your vision becomes more and more blurred as your alcohol consumption continues to increase and your balance and motor skills deteriorate dramatically.

Walking – particularly in a straight line – becomes difficult and stairs can be a particular challenge. At this stage, your emotions can start to be affected too. Some people become aggressive, some become morose. I tend to just sit in a corner quietly chuckling to myself.

Each physical action starts to require more thought – turning your head, picking up your glass, raising it to your mouth – all seem to start requiring a considerable amount of thought and consideration. Speech can be extremely slurred – or in my case – extremely s l o w a n d c o n s i d e r e d...

Compatibility with Driving

It doesn't take a genius to work out that this level of drunkenness is extremely incompatible with driving a car. If you're struggling to walk and talk and pick up a glass, then you'll also struggle with the intricacies of safely controlling a car, looking for hazards and making safe assessments and driving plans. In short, at this stage, you'll be a liability behind the wheel and it's far more likely to be a question of "when" rather than "if" you'll have an accident.

This level of drunkenness is, of course well above any legal drink-drive limit and most judicial systems have sentencing guidelines which would take into account different levels of intoxication and punish offenders accordingly.

Beyond More

Beyond this stage of drunkenness, if you're still able to lift your glass and pour it down your throat, things get really bad.

Your ability to walk and talk is removed, and you're likely to end up in a drunken stupor – on a couch if you're lucky, in the gutter if you're less lucky and in a police cell or hospital bed if you're really unlucky. Alcohol consumption beyond this point can result in unconsciousness and even death.

Compatibility with Driving

Really? This level of drunkenness is pretty much incompatible with life, let alone driving. If you're this drunk and you manage by some miracle to get behind the wheel and start the engine, you'll be lucky if you get past the first lamp-post without an accident.

Incredibly, though, during my police career, I encountered quite a few people who had managed to drive a car at this level of drunkenness.

These people are out there...

How Much Can I Drink and Still Drive?

This is a question I'm asked quite regularly, and people always expect a simple, straightforward answer, like "one pint of lager" or "one glass of wine".

Unfortunately, life (and the human body and chemistry) isn't as simple as that. There are a wide range of different parameters to consider which affect the answer to this question.

Are you male, female, tall, short, fat, thin, a regular or occasional drinker?

Your sex and physical build have a huge effect on your body's ability to process alcohol and on your level of drunkenness for a set amount of alcohol.

Men absorb and process alcohol more efficiently than women and the volume of an individual's body has a huge bearing on how much they will be affected by different amounts of alcohol.

So, if a tall, well-built man drinks a double whisky, it will have a significantly lower effect on his ability to drive than it would on a short, slim woman. It would also raise the woman's blood alcohol level to a much higher degree than the man's due to his larger volume i.e. he's got much more blood in his body than the woman and the alcohol is therefore more diluted by his higher volume of blood.

Regular drinkers build up a level of immunity to alcohol, so if you're a regular or heavy drinker, you'll need to consume more alcohol than an occasional drinker to achieve the same effect. Heavy drinkers, however, need to remain aware that their blood alcohol level will be the same as an occasional drinker's if their body type is similar and they've kept up with each other drink-for-drink. The occasional drinker may feel quite drunk, but the heavy drinker may not feel much effect, but because their blood alcohol levels are the same, the regular, heavy drinker may be well over the limit, even if they feel ok to drive.

What are you Drinking?

Most of you will be aware that different drinks contain different amounts of alcohol, but many people aren't aware of the huge difference in alcohol content between otherwise similar drinks.

In the UK, the alcohol content of drinks is measured as a percentage of the total volume of the drink, so some lagers may be 4% alcohol by volume (ABV) and some Scotch Whiskies may be 40% ABV.

The problem here is that some lagers contain 2.5% ABV and some lagers contain over 9% ABV. So if you were to drink one pint of 9% lager, you're effectively consuming as much alcohol as you would by drinking about 3 ½ pints of 2.5% lager.

Wine can vary between 9% and 16% ABV (but generally sits between 12 and 15%), so the amount of wine you can consume before driving also varies significantly.

Spirits, clearly, have a much higher alcohol content but, again, this content can vary dramatically. Liqueurs start at around 25% ABV, Vodka, rum and Scotch Whisky are usually around 40% ABV, cask strength whisky can be up to 65% ABV and some strong grain spirits, Absinth etc. can be as high as 95% ABV.

These types of drink tend to be consumed in smaller quantities, but the types of mixer you choose can also have a bearing on how much effect certain drinks will have on your body. Mixed with a still mixer, for instance, spirits will be absorbed more slowly in your body than those mixed with a fizzy mixer. So a vodka and orange juice, for instance, will affect you more slowly than a vodka and coke.

You're probably starting to see just how difficult it is to gauge how much you can have to drink and still drive. But there are more things to consider...

How Big?

This might seem obvious, but glass size has a major bearing on how much alcohol you're consuming. Drinking in a pub or other licensed premise, it's easier to keep track of how much alcohol you're drinking. Pub measures are always standard and they even have to (by law!) offer a selection of smaller measures. I've also never, to this day, met a pub landlord who serves in oversize glasses.

At home, however, things are very different. We've a set of wine glasses in our kitchen which will easily hold half-a-bottle of wine each. If I have a glass of single malt, I don't carefully decant it into a Trading Standards approved 25ml measuring thimble. No – I pour out a couple of generous glugs into a glass and add a drop of water. How much alcohol? I've no idea.

So if you drink at home, it's highly likely that you'll generally underestimate the amount of alcohol you're consuming – sometimes to quite an alarming degree.

Anything to Eat Sir?

This may be a concept you're already aware of, but it's worth exploring. If you drink on an empty stomach, your body will absorb the alcohol much more quickly than it does if you drink after a meal.

In other words, go out straight after work and have a few drinks without eating first and you'll be making a fool of yourself much more quickly than if you went for something to eat after work and then have a few drinks.

Relating this situation to something more relevant to this book, if you have a couple of pints on an empty stomach, your driving is likely to be *more* impaired than if you have a couple of pints with a meal.

That's not, of course, to say that you're safe to drive if you've drunk alcohol with a meal – you've still consumed the same *amount* of alcohol and the effects will be similar, it's just that those effects will take longer to show.

That's all Very Interesting – But...

How Much can I Drink and Still Drive?

What? Really? I've just explained to you how complicated this question is to answer and how many variables there are and you *still* want an answer to this question?

The Drink-Drive Limit

Ok then, let's move on to the drink-drive limit and see if that helps us answer the question.

The drink-drive limit in England and Wales is 0.08%. This means that your blood can contain up to 0.08% alcohol before you're not legally allowed to drive. This level was set in 1967 and has not changed since. In 1967, it was felt that 0.08% was the level at which individuals were excessively impaired so that they could not safely control a motor vehicle. Interestingly, more modern research suggests that the actual safe impairment level starts from a blood alcohol level of 0.05%, but more of that shortly.

Most of us are more familiar with the less technical descriptions of the current drink-drive limit in England & Wales:

35 microgrammes of alcohol in 100 millilitres of breath;

80 milligrammes of alcohol in 100 millilitres of blood or;

107 milligrammes of alcohol in 100 millilitres of urine.

Please don't get confused at this stage – the limits listed above are, in reality, all exactly the same and equate to a blood alcohol level of 0.08%. It's just the measurement methods which are different – depending on whether the measurement is taken from a sample of breath, blood or urine.

In reality, the blood and urine levels are becoming increasingly irrelevant as a change in the law in 2015 saw the "statutory option" of having a breath sample replaced with one of blood or urine removed, so the only circumstances these days when blood or urine are used instead of breath would be if the driver were in hospital. (They're probably in hospital because they didn't read this book!).

So how much drink will put me over the limit?

Honestly?

You've just read all the above and you're asking that?

To be honest, I think it's the wrong question anyway – with a blood alcohol level of 0.079%, you may be just under the limit, but your ability to drive will still be impaired. If we go back to the whole purpose of this book, I'm trying to teach you **how not to crash,** and driving whilst impaired – even to a degree that is technically legal – still significantly effects your ability to safely control a car and to make the correct observations and plans involved in driving.

If you want an honest answer to this question, an average sized man could drink one pint of 4% ABV beer or a glass of wine with a meal and still be under the statutory drink-drive limit. For an average sized woman, this amount is slightly less.

But in all honesty – and you probably knew I was leading up to this – the best advice is *don't drink any alcohol before driving a motor vehicle.*

What about the morning after?

Here's another area which some people struggle to understand. If you've had a skinful the night before, there is a strong possibility that you will still be over the drink-drive limit the

following day. And I don't just mean first thing in the morning –
you could still be over the limit well into the afternoon, mostly
dependant on two factors:

1. How much you had to drink, and;

2. When you stopped drinking.

If you go online, you'll find a range of "calculators" which claim
to be able to tell you when you'll be ok to drive again based on
what you've consumed and what time you stopped drinking.

In basic terms, the best advice suggests that it takes your body
an hour to remove each unit of alcohol you've consumed. As an
example, the following is a short list of drinks to demonstrate
how many units they contain:

Pint of 4% ABV draft lager   2.5 Units of Alcohol

Large Glass of 13% ABV Wine   3.5 Units of Alcohol

Double Measure of Scotch at 40% ABV   3 Units of Alcohol

So, if you go out and drink three pints of lager, a glass of wine
and a double whisky, you'll consume 14 units of alcohol. If you
stop drinking at midnight, it'll take your body one hour per unit
to remove the alcohol, so that'll be 14 hours until your body has
removed all the alcohol you consumed.

In other words, it'll be 2.00pm before you can be sure that *all* the
alcohol has been removed from your system.

Now, I'm not suggesting it'll be 2.00pm before you're under the drink-drive limit, because clearly that isn't the case, but it'll be at least 11.00am before you're down to that level and if you start work at 9.00am and set off at 8.00am, then you'll obviously still be well over the limit when you drive to work the next day.

Makes you think doesn't it?

One of the problems is that, after a night's sleep, you often don't actually *feel* drunk when you wake up. You may feel rough, hungover and generally a bit ropey, but you don't usually feel drunk – certainly not in the merry, sociable and enjoyable way that you did the previous evening.

But even though you don't *feel* drunk, the negative effects of the alcohol are still there – the lack of co-ordination, the reduced motor skills, the blurred peripheral vision and the reduced ability to make rational decisions quickly. In other words, all the stuff that affects your ability to drive safely.

In recent years, police forces have reacted to this "morning after" issue by targeting drivers on the morning commute and catching those who were unaware that they still had so much alcohol still sloshing around inside them.

Don't be caught out!

If you have a skinful the night before, assume that you won't be fit to drive until *at least* the early afternoon on the next day, and possibly even later than that if you stopped drinking very late.

Do you Live in Scotland?

If so, lucky you! Mrs Local and I love Scotland – it's a beautiful country with some fantastic driving roads and excellent distilleries – perfect, in other words, for two of my favourite things in life.

The Scottish government has quite a progressive approach to amending its own legislation and it's never shy of sticking its head above the parapet – particularly when it comes to alcohol. They introduced a public-health related licensing objective to their Licensing Act (something the English government has dithered about for years and failed to act on), and they were progressive in looking to introduce a minimum unit price for alcohol (although this one is still stuck in the appeals system somewhere).

In 2014, the Scottish Government took the decision to reduce the drink driving limit in line with more recent advice on impairment levels and safe driving limits. The Scottish drink-drive limit is now 0.05%, which equates to:

22 microgrammes of alcohol in 100 millilitres of breath (35 in rest of UK);

50 milligrammes of alcohol in 100 millilitres of blood (80 in rest of UK) or;

67 milligrammes of alcohol in 100 millilitres of urine (107 in rest of UK).

So the advice I gave above for England and Wales should be reduced as follows:

An average sized man could drink half a pint of 4% ABV beer or a small glass of wine with a meal and still be under the statutory drink-drive limit in Scotland. For an average sized woman, this amount is slightly less.

But in all honesty, in Scotland, if you want to remain under the drink-drive limit, I would have to advise not drinking at all before driving a motor vehicle. The same additional caution should be applied to morning-after drinking north of the border too.

In other words, if you refer to new year as "Hogmanay", enjoy eating stuffed sheep's stomach and use the word "wee" a lot in a non-toilet capacity, then you should really avoid driving altogether on the day after a heavy night out.

To Summarise

Drink-Driving can be a very emotive issue and there are a wide range of opposing opinions about the subject, ranging from teetotal temperance societies, through support groups for bereaved families and some of the old-fashioned views often expressed by (mostly) older people "I don't see the harm if I'm only going half-a-mile".

In terms of avoiding an accident, the advice is simple – if you don't consume any alcohol at all before driving, you'll keep your chances of having an accident to a minimum.

If you do consume alcohol – even a small amount – then your chances of having an accident are much higher.

We all know the possible consequences – hospital, police station, driving ban, prison, mortuary – I don't think I need to labour those points.

If you do have a drink on a night out, just remember that a taxi is always – *always* – cheaper than a drink-drive conviction.

It's not Just You!

Remember as well, that it doesn't matter how responsible or sober you are, there are still plenty of other people out there who are willing to risk driving after a few drinks. I've had to break the news to quite a few families that a loved one has been killed by one of these drivers and each of those conversations has stayed with me ever since.

This may be obvious, but there are times and places where you're more likely to encounter a drunk driver – between 11.00pm and 5.00am when licensed premises are closing, people are more likely to be driving home after a few, and that likelihood is significantly higher in rural areas than in urban areas. If you live in the country, the temptation to drive after a few drinks seems to be higher because of a perceived lack of taxis and the belief that there is much less chance of seeing a police car and getting caught.

When you're driving at these times, be wary of vehicles approaching junctions to your left and right as they may not give way to you – move away from the junctions slightly on the approach and be prepared to brake or avoid if the car pulls out.

You may have a mental image of a drunk driver – weaving down the road, bumping off kerbs and crossing the white line whilst driving at 15mph. I've seen a few drunk drivers like this, but generally the signs are much subtler and not as easy to spot.

Someone who has had a drink will often overcompensate for their level of intoxication, so someone driving carefully at, or just under the speed limit and obeying every traffic sign and road marking can often be an indication that they've had a drink.

Others have a level of overconfidence and – particularly if they've got passengers in the car – will drive excessively fast for the road and traffic conditions. These are easier to spot!

The more difficult drink-drivers to spot and avoid are the functioning alcoholics who need a drink in order to operate at a level which everyone else considers to be normal. These people need a drink before they leave the house in the morning and continually need a drink during the day. They may be driving whilst intoxicated at any time of the day or night. I've dealt with people who were drunk in the morning on their way to work, dropping their children off at school and even – once – whilst driving a taxi full of passengers.

If you spot a car which you think may be driven by someone who is drunk, my best advice is to invoke Reg's policy on non-involvement. In other words, stay well away from them, avoid getting too close or overtaking them and don't give them an opportunity to involve you in their next accident or incident.

By all means report them to the police if you like – you can use your mobile phone in an emergency and preventing a serious accident would certainly be classed as an emergency, so ring 999 if you like and give a description of the vehicle and its location & direction of travel. I know some people don't like reporting things like this to the police and that's a position I understand and respect to a certain degree.

But if someone had done just that back in 1994, I'd probably still have a sister.

Driver/Rider impaired by drugs (illicit or medicinal) 1%

You would think, wouldn't you, with all the publicity we've seen recently on the dangers of driving under the influence of drugs, that hundreds of people were being killed and maimed every year by drivers smacked off their heads on coke and meth?

It may come as something of a surprise then, that, in fact, only 684 accidents (out of over 115,000) were judged to be caused by a driver who was under the influence of drugs – that's just over 0.5% of all accidents. Like drink driving, however, the percentage of fatalities from those accidents was higher – 47 people died as a result of drug/driving in 2014, which is 3% of all fatalities, but still, perhaps, not as high a figure as you might think – especially when compared with almost 500 who die as a result of someone losing control of their vehicle.

However, drugs – whether you like it or not – are now a well-established part of our society and many hundreds of thousands of people regularly use recreational drugs, either as part of their social life or at home. As such, I thought it would be useful to include some genuine facts and information about drug use and driving, without being judgemental or sanctimonious.

I'll look at the effects of various drugs, whether those effects are compatible with driving and then give some clear guidance on whether you should drive after taking them. I've included the drugs I consider to be the most common recreational drugs in the UK at the moment, together with a small selection of less common drugs.

I appreciate that there are many more drugs in use than those I've listed and that there are many variations on some of the ones I have listed, but I've tried to keep the list as relevant to as many people as possible, so my apologies if I've missed out your favourite drug of choice.

Recreational Drugs

Cannabis

I've heard lots of rubbish spouted about cannabis over the years. At one end of the spectrum are people who believe it's less harmful than tap water and should be available to nursing mothers and pensioners free of charge. At the other end are those who believe it's chronically addictive, poisonous and a gateway drug which will lead to years of heroin addiction and then death in a graffiti-strewn crack den.

These extreme views are mostly rubbish. The truth is that cannabis is probably the most widely used of all illegal recreational drugs and – by itself – it is relatively safe. By "relatively safe", I mean that there are no recorded instances of anyone dying as a direct result of consuming cannabis.

People have died whilst under the influence of cannabis, of course, and there are obvious health risks associated with smoking tobacco mixed with cannabis, but cannabis on its own actually has a very low toxicity and no-one has ever died of a cannabis overdose.

There are, however, some potentially very serious side effects of cannabis use and it can have a very serious and long-lasting detrimental effect on your mental health.

In the UK, cannabis is illegal and you can be prosecuted for possession or for supplying. Many people are of the view that it has been "legalised" in the UK, but that isn't the case – in 2003, the Government downgraded cannabis from a class B to a class C drug, meaning that the penalties for possession and supply were reduced. In 2009, the Government reversed this decision and re-classified cannabis as a class B drug. To this day, I'm unsure what they were smoking…

Cannabis comes in a number of different forms – resin, leaves, buds (herbal cannabis) & oil and is most commonly consumed either by smoking or eating (usually when used as an ingredient in something else like a cake, pizza etc.).

Effects

Like alcohol, cannabis is – clinically – a depressant, which means that it slows down the functions of your brain and central nervous system. For many people it can also act as a mild hallucinogenic. The immediate effects of cannabis include a loss of inhibition, spontaneous laughter (at pretty much anything), altered perception of sound & colour, reduced coordination, increased heart rate and a feeling of relaxation.

Perception of sensations can be affected, particularly sound and vision – colours can be distorted and vision can become blurred and things can appear different or odd.

It is much more difficult to concentrate after consuming cannabis and many people experience feelings of paranoia and/or confusion. In addition, balance is affected, as is the ability to make sensible, considered decisions.

You may have tried cannabis and experienced some of these effects. You may know someone who regularly uses cannabis and tells you only about the nicer effects of the drug, or you may be a regular user and completely disagree with my list of effects – all of that is fine, but here are the problems with cannabis...

Firstly, the strength of cannabis varies greatly. 20 years ago, most cannabis was imported from abroad, usually in resin form. It wasn't excessively strong, but the strength was generally consistent wherever you bought it from.

These days, the vast majority of cannabis sold in the UK is grown in the UK, in operations ranging from small grows in the loft, through to large, commercial cannabis farms growing thousands of plants. It tends to be sold in herbal form these days and the strength of some of these home-grown strains can be much, *much* higher than imported cannabis resin. In some cases, home-grown or UK supplied herbal cannabis can be up to 20 times as potent as imported cannabis resin.

Now, this might not be so bad if cannabis was sold and labelled in a similar manner as alcohol. If you could look at the packet and see the strength like you can with lager, for instance, you'd easily be able to tell if you were buying the weed equivalent of Miller Light, or Kestrel Super.

But, of course, it isn't sold like that because it's illegal. You have to buy it from a dealer who will always tell you simply that it's really good stuff, and you'll have no idea as to how potent it is. So deciding how much to use is very difficult and people tend to just take cannabis until they are feeling the effects.

How you take it has a major bearing on the effects as well. Smoking cannabis gives you the effects almost immediately, so it's reasonably easy to moderate your consumption and stop smoking once you've reached a level of high that you're comfortable with.

If cannabis is eaten, however, the story is very different. It can take up to 45 minutes for your body to digest a cake to the point where the cannabis starts to have an effect. So you can eat a cake, feel no effects whatsoever for ½ an hour, decide to have another cake, and then suddenly find that the effects are kicking in with a vengeance before you've even started digesting the second cake.

And, of course, you can't stop digesting once you've started, so you're stuck with the effects of however much you've consumed until they eventually wear off.

Cannabis & Driving

Many of the effects described above are incompatible with the safe control of a motor vehicle. Your brain functions are depressed and slowed by the effects of cannabis and as such your reaction times will be reduced. Motor functions and hand-eye coordination can be seriously affected and it's much more difficult to concentrate on the physical and mental skills involved in driving.

Combine these effects with the loss of inhibitions and – in some cases – increased confidence that cannabis can bring, and there is a higher likelihood that you'll think your driving will be better and therefore take the decision to drive when you're unfit to do so.

It's common for drivers who are under the effects of cannabis to overcompensate for their intoxication and drive more slowly to compensate for their reduced reaction times and slower perceptions. This in itself brings significant risks and an overcompensating driver will also assume that they're safer – when, of course, they're not.

So to answer the inevitable question – should I drive when I've taken cannabis? – quite simply, no, you shouldn't.

Even if you're an experienced and long-term cannabis user and you may feel that you're fine to drive after smoking some weed, it's still having an effect on your ability to drive even if you don't feel like it is, so if you want to reduce your chances of having an accident, then avoid driving altogether when you're using cannabis.

Another difficulty is that there's no "limit" for cannabis like there is for alcohol, so again, it's impossible to judge your level of intoxication in comparison with an acknowledged level of consumption.

The Morning (or evening, or afternoon) After

If you've taken cannabis, how long will it be before you can drive again?

As with alcohol, this is a very difficult one to answer, as it depends on many variables, such as your level of consumption, whether you've eaten, slept, drank anything, your height & build etc.

The immediate effects of cannabis (the "high") will generally last for 3-5 hours if you've been smoking weed, and considerably longer if you've eaten it. That's not to say, however, that you'll be safe to drive after 5 hours – just that the immediate effects will have worn off at that point.

One surprising fact is just how long the chemical constituents of cannabis (called cannabinoids) stay in your system for. Cannabis can be detected in your blood or urine for up to 6 weeks after you've taken it. That's not to say you'll be impaired by cannabis for 6 weeks – just that it can still be detected for 6 weeks, which is something to consider if you work in a job which requires drug testing.

My best advice if you've taken cannabis is to leave it a full 24 hours before you drive.

That may sound like a long time, but remember all the stuff I wrote about differing strengths and consumption and it'll make sense. Remember that it won't be out of your system after 24 hours, but the effects should have worn off by then.

Please be careful though – use this advice as guidance only. Be sensible in your consumption & try to leave as long as you possibly can between taking cannabis and driving.

Cocaine

Unlike alcohol and cannabis, cocaine is a stimulant, which means that it stimulates your brain and nervous system and gives the user a fast blast of confidence and euphoria.

Judging the strength – or purity – of cocaine can be very difficult, if not impossible. Remember that this stuff is imported and sold by criminals – people who aren't concerned about their commercial reputation or whether they'll get a bad review on Amazon.

Without that concern about reputation, the dealers will look to maximise their profit from every gram of coke they sell, so most cocaine bought for consumption in the UK is diluted down to a strength of around 10 to 15%. So the other 85 to 90% of that white powder you're shoving up your nose will be talcum powder, flour, glucose powder, washing powder or scouring powder.

Good profit for the dealers then, but not such good news for your nasal cavity and, of course, very difficult for you to judge your level of intoxication.

Cocaine used to be the preserve of the rich and famous, but massive increases in production and importation during the 1990s and 2000s brought with it a dramatic reduction in price and many people now view coke as a fairly normal part of a night out. I think they'd feel differently if they saw how the stuff was made and what it's cut with, but I said I wouldn't be judgemental, so I'll just stick to the facts.

Cocaine is classified as a "class A" drug in the UK – the most serious classification.

The Effects

The short term effects of cocaine are that it gives a quick euphoric high – confidence soars, heart rate increases dramatically, and users generally feel a huge "rush" of energy and confidence. Alongside these effects, some users can become more aggressive, impatient and have a tendency to make rash and ill-considered decisions.

These initial effects can be quite short-lived, but such is the nature of cocaine, once they have worn off, users tend to want more, as soon as possible. It's been described as "very moreish". As such, consumption can continue all night, particularly as the effects of the drug mask tiredness and allows users to carry on partying all night.

Cocaine and Driving

Clearly these short-term effects are incompatible with driving. Drivers who have taken coke tend to drive excessively fast and overestimate their own ability. It's common for drivers high on coke to lose control of their vehicle due to these effects.

The sense of overconfidence that cocaine brings means that individuals who have taken coke are more likely to make the decision to drive, thinking not only that they're ok to drive, but even that their driving ability is enhanced by the coke.

Studies have shown that cocaine can slightly increase reaction times, but many years of advanced driver training and road policing have taught me that good reaction times do not make for a good driver. Just the opposite in many cases. 17 and 18 year olds, for instance, have much faster reaction times than people in their 40's, but have many more accidents due to a lack of experience and overconfidence.

The driver on coke, however, is likely to feel that their driving abilities are enhanced by the drug, which can lead to some very poor decision making.

The Morning After

The "high" effects of cocaine generally only last between ½ an hour and an hour, so you may think that, given a couple of hours you'll be safe to drive. The problem is that, once consumption stops, users can experience a significant "crash" when they feel exhausted and struggle to stay awake. So although it's fairly obvious that driving immediately after taking coke should be avoided, the "come down" period after consumption is also a very dangerous time to get behind the wheel.

My advice is to leave it at least 24 hours before driving if you've taken cocaine.

It's also worth noting that cocaine can mask the effects of alcohol, so if you drink whilst you're taking coke, you may feel as though the alcohol isn't having an effect, when, in fact, it is, and that effect will last longer than the coke and drunkenness could hit you up to several hours after you've stopped drinking.

Amphetamines

Like Cocaine, Amphetamines or Speed is a stimulant, usually supplied in powder form and taken by snorting or consuming in a drink. Speed is also a very common drug these days and many people take it regularly – particularly when going out for the evening. Speed is a class B drug in the UK.

Effects

Speed gives the user an adrenaline rush – it wakes you up and raises your heart rate and blood pressure. It raises the user's confidence, removes their inhibitions, makes them more outgoing and extrovert.

It can also give you a very dry mouth and in many people, speed masks the effects of alcohol, so if it's taken before, or during a night out, a user is far more likely to drink more than they normally would without the speed.

Speed and Driving

Some of the negative effects of speed include disorientation, an increased tendency to take risks, lack of coordination, lapses in concentration, and aggression.

Speed can also make people feel overconfident in their own abilities – including their driving abilities – which, of course, increases the likelihood that someone will chose to drive having taken speed.

The mixture of alcohol and speed can be particularly dangerous, because, although you may not feel like the alcohol is having any effects on you, it most certainly is, and your driving will still be grossly impaired as a result.

The Morning After

Or should I say the day after? Or even the evening after? Speed is likely to keep you up partying all night, but the come-down from the drug can hit you like a train. Once the effects wear off, fatigue will kick in very quickly and if you've been drinking, you'll also start to feel the effects of the drink, which will, of course, increase your fatigue even further.

In short, you'll want to sleep, and you'll find it very difficult, if not impossible, to avoid nodding off wherever you are when the crash hits you.

So you really don't want to be at the wheel of a car when it does...

My advice is to leave it *at least* 24 hours before driving if you've taken speed. You may well need to leave it even longer – be honest with yourself about how you're feeling and don't drive unless you're certain that the effects have worn off *and* you've had enough rest.

MDMA/Ecstasy

Ecstasy is a strong stimulant drug which usually comes in the form of a pill. It can make you feel relaxed, very happy and uplifted, usually with an overwhelming urge to dance. It's very common and estimates on the numbers of users are as high as several hundred thousand people per week. You may also be surprised to learn that ecstasy is a class A drug in the UK, alongside heroin, cocaine etc.

Effects

Most ecstasy users will only ever tell you about the positive effects of the drug. They will tell you that it relaxes you, helps you lose all sense of self-consciousness, makes you feel extremely happy and sociable and give you a huge lift. They'll also tell you that some people can hallucinate to a small degree, and that light and colours can seem enhanced, together with changes in perception.

What they're unlikely to tell you about, however, are some of the negative effects of the drug – the distortion of perception, thinking, and memory; the slowing of your reactions and disorientation; the anxiety and alteration of your perception.

Ecstasy and Driving

Clearly, these effects are highly incompatible with safely driving a motor vehicle, but as with some other stimulant drugs, ecstasy can also increase your confidence and make you think you're perfectly safe to drive – or even *safer* at driving than when you're completely straight. This overconfidence also means that drivers who have taken ecstasy are more likely to make rash decisions and to take greater risks when they do drive.

I've met many people who think they're absolutely fine to drive after taking ecstasy – mainly due to the fact that most people don't drink alcohol when they're on E.

They're wrong.

Best advice if you're taking ecstasy is to make sure you leave your car and keys at home and don't give in to the temptation to drive when you've had one or two pills.

The Morning After

Clinical studies have shown that ecstasy (and similar derivatives of MDMA – MDA, MDEA etc.) can have an effect on your body for between 3 and 10 hours. The problem is – as with most other drugs purchased from dealers – you've no idea of the strength of the pills you've bought, so you've therefore no clear idea how long the effects will last for.

In addition, the duration and intensity of the effects depend on a wide variety of factors, which will vary from person-to-person, so a prediction on how long effects will last is very difficult to make. It's also very difficult for a person who has taken ecstasy to judge when the effects have fully worn off, so the only safe way to ensure that you are no longer impaired is to leave a good, long period of time before driving again.

In addition to the effects of the ecstasy itself, the come-down from the drug can be exhausting, and fatigue – as I've explored elsewhere in this chapter – can be just as dangerous and debilitating as taking drugs or drinking alcohol. So you'll need a good, long period of rest *after the effects of ecstasy have worn off* before you're safe to drive again

It may seem like this is becoming my standard answer, but you should wait at least 24 hours after taking ecstasy before getting behind the wheel.

Heroin / Opiates

I appreciate that not many of you are regular users of heroin or other opiate-based drugs, but I'm also not naïve enough to think that there aren't still a substantial number of people who regularly use heroin, and a much larger number of people who may be tempted to try it once or use it occasionally.

I know many of you may have a mental image of heroin users as Trainspotting bag-head types, but I've met many people over the years who live relatively normal lives whilst maintaining a heroin habit. There are also a large number of heroin users who let the drug completely take over their lives, to the exclusion of pretty much everything else.

Having said all that, I mentioned earlier that I wasn't trying to be judgemental in any way, so I'll stuck to the facts about the drug, its effects and compatibility with driving.

Heroin is an opiate drug derived from a particular strain of poppy and is usually supplied in powder form. It can be smoked, snorted or injected and it is extremely addictive for many people. Heroin is a class A drug in the UK

The Effects

Heroin is a depressant drug which induces an initial sleepy euphoria and total relief from stress and anxiety as the drug enters the system. These initial feelings then lead on to a feeling of calm and relaxation.

These are the pleasant effects that most regular users will tell you about and which they seek to experience every time they use the drug. The problem is, the more you use heroin, the more your body builds up a tolerance – and a *reliance* - on the drug and the more you need to use it to achieve those pleasant effects.

Heavy users can very quickly get to the point where they feel as though they need heroin just to feel normal – at this point the addiction has well and truly set in.

I'm not suggesting that every heroin user is an addict, or that every user is overwhelmingly driven by the desire for more heroin, but this is a very common pattern and one you should be aware of if you're ever tempted to try it.

The come-down from heroin can be hugely variable – some people will recover from a single or occasional use with very few ill effects. Others – particularly heavier users – will experience a very unpleasant withdrawal period as their body craves more heroin. Cold Turkey, clucking, call it what you will – is a very nasty experience and anyone going through it will feel as though they are dying from a combination of nausea, diarrhoea, hot and cold sweats, joint pain, muscle cramps, confusion and an almost overwhelming craving for more heroin.

Heroin and Driving

Some of the effects of heroin are particularly incompatible with driving. Slow reaction times, taking longer to respond to events or situations, reduced coordination, an inability to think clearly, blurred vision, drowsiness & a tendency to nod off and even nausea and vomiting.

A person who has been using heroin may have a tendency to think that - if they are especially careful - they will be able to drive safely. However, the drug may have affected their view and experience of reality, and their judgement. Their actions and responses will be impaired, but they may not be aware of how much their driving skills have been affected.

The Morning After

The effects of the drug can last up to 24 hours, and you should then also factor in a recovery period when you should rest and allow your body to fully recover.

For a single or occasional user, my advice is to wait *at least* 36 hours after taking heroin before you drive again.

For heavy users or addicts, this may sound harsh, but you should avoid driving altogether. If you're an addict, your body is constantly going through a cycle of experiencing the effects of heroin, suffering withdrawal and then back to experiencing the effects again. In short, you'll never be fit to drive safely whilst you're going through this cycle.

If you choose to break the cycle and come off heroin, withdrawal can last up to 7 days. – the symptoms will peak at around 3 days and be subsiding after 5 or so, but it'll be a full 7 days before someone is fully recovered from heroin withdrawal. As such, if you're a heavy user or addicted, you should leave it a full week before you contemplate driving again.

LSD

LSD or Acid is a very powerful hallucinogenic drug which is usually supplied as doses on small squares of paper or small pellets. Its effects vary dramatically from user to user and it can be very difficult to predict how different people will respond to the drug. Some people report very positive, uplifting effects, whilst others can experience some extremely frightening and disorientating effects. It can also have a long-lasting negative effect on some people's mental health (especially if you have a history of mental health problems) – sometimes many years after even a single use, so please make sure you are fully aware of the risks when considering taking LSD.

LSD is a class A drug in the UK.

The Effects

Acid is a hallucinogenic drug, which means that it alters your perception of the world, your vision, hearing and other senses. Users can experience a distorted sense of reality, colours and sounds can appear like pulsating patterns and some people report that their senses feel as though they are mixing together.

Emotions can be heightened by acid, and its good advice to be aware of your emotional state before taking it – if you're feeling anxious, for example, or angry, the acid will exaggerate those emotions and you could be in danger as a result. Best advice is never to take it when you're alone and have some friends around you to look after you if you do.

A "bad trip" can be an extremely frightening and shocking experience and your behaviour can be extremely unpredictable whilst experiencing a bad trip.

Another word of caution – acid can sometimes take up to 90 minutes to have an effect, so don't be tempted to take more if you don't feel as though it's working as the chances are you'll end up taking far too much if you do.

LSD and Driving

These effects are clearly extremely incompatible with driving safely – I wouldn't let you have a go with my Scalextric if you'd taken acid, let alone drive a car on the road.

With an altered sense of reality, distorted vision, hallucinations and roller-coaster emotions, you're in no state whatsoever to make the rational decisions associated with safely controlling a car and the likelihood of an accident if you drive on acid is extremely high. So please – don't!

The Morning After

How long before the acid wears off? As with many drugs, this is dependent on a number of different variables, so I'll give you a very conservative answer. After a single dose, it can be anything up to 14 hours before the effects completely cease. Of course, after a trip, you'll be tired and this can also negatively affect your ability to drive, so you'll need a good long rest before you're completely fit to drive.

So you should leave it an absolute minimum of 24 hours before driving if you've taken LSD – and longer if possible, just to be sure you're not affected in any way.

Magic Mushrooms / Psilocybin Mushrooms

There are around 12 different types of hallucinogenic mushrooms which grow wild in the UK, the most common being the Liberty Cap. Mushrooms are usually eaten, made into a drink, or dried for use later.

The effects of mushrooms are very similar to the effects of LSD/acid. Small doses can bring on excitement and euphoria, while bigger doses (15 small mushrooms or more) can bring on shape and colour distortions, vivid hallucinations and enhanced sensory feelings.

Although they may seem relatively benign, magic mushrooms can be extremely strong and are classified as a class A drug in the UK.

The Effects

Mushrooms have a very similar hallucinogenic effect to LSD/acid. As with acid, trips can be good or bad and it's never easy to know how much to take or how strong mushrooms will be.

Mushrooms and Driving

Mushrooms can distort colours, sounds and vision. They can make a user feel as if their senses are mixed up so that, for example, they think they can hear colours and see sounds. Mushrooms can make users feel as though they are in a "waking dream" and can speed up or slow down their sense of time.

These effects are extremely incompatible with driving a car and you should avoid driving, or even having access to a car if you're going to use magic mushrooms.

Mushrooms can take up to 2 hours to take effect – this is very important as you may take some, think they're not having an effect and then drive your car, just as the mushrooms start to take effect. If you've taken some mushrooms, assume they will have an effect even if you're not aware of it and avoid driving.

The Morning After

The hallucinogenic effects of magic mushrooms can last much longer than you might expect – it's common for the effects to last up to 6 hours and sometimes as long as 12 hours.

If you then take into account the inevitable consequences of fatigue, it seems clear that you shouldn't contemplate driving for at least 24 hours after taking magic mushrooms.

Ketamine

Ketamine is a very strong short-acting anesthetic which most commonly comes in powder form, but can also be supplied in liquid and tablet form. It is a very important medicinal drug, used by health professionals around the world for its anesthetic properties.

It is also commonly used as a recreational drug – it can be snorted, injected or ingested and is classified as a class B drug in the UK.

The Effects

Ketamine is very fast acting, and within around 20 minutes of taking it, users report a very intense "rush" followed by powerful hallucinations and sometimes out of body experiences, along with physical incapacitation (it is, of course, an anaesthetic).

Some people can be completely paralysed by ketamine and unable to speak, whilst others either feel sick or throw up.

Because it's an anaesthetic, you need to be careful when taking ketamine because it's quite possible for you to injure yourself and not realise because you can't feel the pain.

Ketamine and Driving

You don't need to be a qualified chemist to work out that driving after taking a powerful anaesthetic is a really bad idea.

With hallucinations, incapacitation, paralysis and an inability to communicate, driving should be the last thing on your mind, so please avoid driving at all costs if you're intending to take ketamine.

The Morning After

The immediate effects of ketamine will wear off within 3-4 hours, but for around 24 hours after taking ketamine, users can experience memory loss, impaired judgement, disorientation, clumsiness, aches and pains and depression.

Best advice is therefore to leave it a little longer than 24 hours before driving if you've taken ketamine – I'd suggest 36 hours to ensure that you're no longer affected in any way, and that you're fully rested and recovered.

Methamphetamine

Far more common in the US than the UK, but nevertheless available in the UK if you look hard enough, Methamphetamine, Crystal Meth, Meth, Crystal, Ice or any number of other pseudonyms, is an extremely addictive stimulant drug which is chemically similar to amphetamine. It takes the form of a white, odorless, crystalline powder

Those of you who have seen "Breaking Bad" will be familiar with Crystal Meth and the dangerous chemicals which go into its production. It can be inhaled, smoked or injected and is very addictive – even after only a few doses.

The Effects

Methamphetamine takes effect almost immediately and produces an immediate, intense euphoria. It can be taken orally, smoked, snorted, or dissolved in water or alcohol and injected. The euphoric high can wear off very quickly, meaning that users can fall very quickly into a pattern of very frequent drug-taking. The drug increases the production of dopamine, which is the body's own "pleasure" chemical and is linked to the drugs high addictiveness.

Meth can cause agitation, an inability to focus attention on multiple tasks, inattention, restlessness, increased reaction time, time distortion, depressed reflexes, poor balance and coordination, and an inability to follow directions.

Meth and Driving

Just have a second look at that last paragraph – does that sound like a list of attributes which are compatible with the safe use of a motor vehicle? No, of course it doesn't, so if you're daft enough to try – or use – methamphetamine, you should avoid driving completely. If you're addicted to the drug or using it regularly, then you should completely avoid driving altogether.

The Morning After

The immediate effects of meth can take up to 24 hours, but the chemical constituents of the drug can remain in your body for up to 10 days, so it is advisable to avoid driving for at least a week after your last dose of meth. You may feel like you're fine to drive after a day or so, but the drug can still have an effect on you so it is advisable to wait the full week before driving again.

Anabolic Steroids

Unlike most other drugs I've looked at in this section, anabolic steroids aren't taken to provide any kind of short-term effect or "high". They are a drug which mimic certain natural hormones which regulate how the body grows and develops. Steroids are a Class C drug and can only be sold by pharmacists with a doctor's prescription.

The Effects

Steroids are increasingly used by people who want to improve their physical appearance, build muscle and increase their physical size. When used as part of a training regime, they encourage accelerated muscle growth and are particularly popular amongst men in their early-to-mid 20's.

Steroids can be prescribed for use in dealing with a wide range of medical issues, but the steroids used by those who want to improve their appearance are commonly supplied illegally and the doses are not carefully monitored.

As well as the less desirable physical effects of steroid use – shrunken testicles, breast growth in men, body hair growth in women, infertility and raised blood pressure – in many people it can have a significant negative effect on their moods, making them aggressive and irritable.

Steroids and Driving

It's this increase in irritability and aggression which can be incompatible with driving. Heavy steroid users can fly off the handle with very little provocation into a "roid rage" which is often, to those who know them well, out of character.

These aggressive outbursts can easily affect your judgement if you're driving. We all know how easy it is to be wound up and upset by other people's poor driving, but if your mood is influenced by excessive steroid use, these episodes can explode out of all proportion. It's not unheard of for steroid users to become involved in extremely serious road-rage type incidents and people have been seriously hurt and even killed in these incidents.

My advice is to avoid driving altogether if you're using anabolic steroids.

If you choose to ignore this advice, you should monitor your moods very carefully, and if you feel your levels of anger and aggression rising, you should stop and take a break as soon as possible to avoid your changing mood becoming a full-on "hulk" moment.

Glue & Solvents

You may think that glue sniffing was a 1970's fad which went out with flared trousers and the Bay City Rollers, but you'd be wrong. Glue and solvent abuse is alive and well in the UK & although it isn't publicised very widely, there are a significant number of people in the UK who inhale glue, household solvents, butane gas, petrol and other chemicals as recreational intoxicants.

The Effects

Solvents provide a very strong feeling of intoxication almost immediately which can sometimes be accompanied by hallucinations.

Users can appear dazed and unsteady with slurred speech and unpredictable behaviour. There is a real risk of vomiting, choking and possibly unconsciousness.

Glue and Driving

Solvents can have a severe effect on your ability to make sensible, rational decisions and users are very likely to take dangerous risks that they would never contemplate when sober.

With this decreased ability to assess risks, combined with heavy intoxication and hallucinations, it almost goes without saying that solvent or glue use is highly incompatible with driving a car.

The Morning After

The effects of glue and solvents wear off after only about 45 minutes to an hour. The long-term health risks, however, are far more concerning and you should really have a serious think about your life if you're using solvents on a regular basis.

My advice would be to avoid driving altogether when you're using and leave it a full day before you consider driving.

Tranquilisers/Barbiturates

Benzodiazepines are prescribed drugs for reducing stress and anxiety, promoting calmness, relaxation and sleep and as anti-depressants. The most common benzodiazepine is Temazepam, but there are a range of other similar drugs which usually come in tablet form.

The Effects

The most debilitating effects of these drugs are forgetfulness, confusion and drowsiness.

Benzodiazepines and Driving

Drowsiness and confusion are clearly two effects which are incompatible with driving a motor vehicle. The drowsiness is very hard to fight and, depending on how many pills you've taken, can take effect very quickly. I've explored fatigue and the dangers of driving whilst tired later in this chapter, but it's clear that driving whilst under the influence of these types of drugs is very risky indeed.

The Morning After

Studies have shown that Benzodiazepines can have a negative effect on your ability to drive for up to 9.5 hours after taking the drug. To be on the safe side, my advice would be to leave it a minimum of 12 hours after taking these drugs before driving again – and if you've taken a large dose, I'd leave it 24 hours.

Mephedrone

Mephedrone (Meow-Meow) is a powerful stimulant drug, closely related to amphetamine, methamphetamine and ecstasy. It generally comes in powder form and is taken by being snorted, dabbed (ingested) or injected. Mephedrone is a class B drug in the UK.

The Effects

Mephedrone induces feelings of euphoria, alertness and affection towards others. It can also make you feel anxious and paranoid and it can overstimulate your heart, circulation and nervous system, with a real risk of inducing fits.

The effects are often described as a mix between amphetamines, ecstasy and cocaine. It can make you feel alert, confident, talkative and euphoric, but it can also make users feel sick, paranoid and anxious, and it can cause vomiting and headaches.

Other reported effects include heart palpitations, insomnia, loss of short-term memory, vertigo, grinding of teeth, sweating and uncomfortable changes in body temperature.

Mephedrone and Driving

I don't think you need to be a biochemist to work out for yourself that these effects are completely incompatible with the safe control of a motor vehicle. If you're using Mephedrone, there is no way that you should even contemplate driving a car.

The Morning After

Studies suggest that you can still be under the influence of Mephedrone up to 24 hours after taking the drug. In order to ensure that you are no longer impaired, you should leave it *at least* 48 hours before you get behind the wheel if you've been using Mephedrone.

GHB

GHB (GammaHydroxyButyrate) or liquid ecstasy is an increasingly popular drug which has similar effects to alcohol. It is supplied in liquid form and is classified as a class C drug in the UK.

The Effects

In small doses, GHB can make you feel uninhibited, exhilarated, relaxed and feeling good. Larger doses can lead to disorientation, nausea, a numbing of the muscles or muscle spasms and vomiting.

GHB and Driving

Further effects of GHB include impaired balance and coordination, dizziness, blurred or distorted vision, loss of peripheral vision, uncontrollable vomiting, and cognitive effects including confusion, sedation, agitation, distractibility, and impaired judgment and decision-making.

Does this sound like a good mix with driving a motor vehicle safely? No, of course it doesn't. Add into the mix that users can become suddenly and unexpectedly unconscious, and you've got a disastrous combination if you decide to be daft enough to drive on GHB.

If you've ever encountered someone on GHB, you may think they are drunk – they will be unsteady on their feet, unpredictable in their movements and uninhibited in their behaviour. Quite simply, you should never mix GHB and driving.

The Morning After

The primary effects of GHB last approximately 1.5 to 2 hours. Some users report feeling the effects at a lower level for a further 2 or 3 hours. This, however, is all dependant on how much you've taken and over what period of time. Some users tend to take GHB "little and often" during the evening, in which case the effects will last considerably longer than if you've just taken a single dose at the start of the night.

Another consideration with GHB is that when the GHB wears off, a "dopamine rebound" can occur. This is essentially a flush of accumulated levels of dopamine being released in the nervous system. And can cause middle-of-the-night awakenings. It can also cause general feelings of increased well-being, alertness and arousal the next day.

With these facts in mind, you should leave it *at least* 24 hours from your last dose of GHB before you consider driving again. And if you're in any doubt as to whether you're still affected, you should leave it even longer,

Synthetic Cannabis/Spice etc.

Synthetic Cannabis, commonly referred to as "Spice" is a drug which sits within a group of drugs which have come to be known in the UK as "legal highs". "Legal" refers to the fact that possession or supply of these types of drugs is not prohibited, although, at the time of writing, a new piece of legislation – The Psychoactive Substances Act – is about to be introduced in the UK, making these types of drugs illegal.

Synthetic Cannabis is basically dried and ground-up plant matter, sprayed with a chemical compound called "synthetic cannabinoids". Cannabinoids are the chemical constituent of cannabis which cause the user to experience a "high", and it's now possible to recreate these cannabinoids artificially in a lab.

They are taken in the same way that cannabis is taken and the problem with these drugs is that, although they have traditionally been sold and supplied perfectly legally in the UK, their effects can be far more potent and unpredictable than actual cannabis.

The Effects

Synthetic Cannabis can cause an elevated mood, relaxation and altered perception. It can also cause symptoms of psychosis, extreme anxiety, confusion, paranoia and hallucinations.

Other effects include a rapid heart rate, vomiting, violent behavior and suicidal thoughts. It can also raise blood pressure and cause reduced blood supply to the heart, as well as kidney damage and seizures.

Synthetic Cannabis and Driving

Come on – you know what I'm going to say, don't you?! We explored cannabis earlier in this chapter and looked in detail at why using cannabis is incompatible with safe driving. With synthetic cannabis, the effects are far more unpredictable and therefore it's even more incompatible with driving than real cannabis.

The Morning After

As with cannabis, my best advice if you've taken synthetic cannabis is to leave it a full 24 hours before you drive.

That may sound like a long time, but remember all the stuff about unknown strengths and consumption and it'll make sense. Remember that it won't be out of your system after 24 hours, but the effects should have worn off by then.

Legal Highs/Research chemicals/2C

In addition to synthetic cannabis, there are an increasingly wide range of "legal highs" available in the UK, which are designed to mimic the effects of a wide range of different drugs, from cocaine to Viagra.

As with synthetic cannabis, the Psychoactive Substances Bill will make these drugs illegal around the time that this book is published, but the fact that these drugs have been legally supplied by shops and dealers for the past few years has led to a common belief that these drugs are somehow harmless and benign.

This belief couldn't be further from the truth – although previously legally supplied, they are commonly labelled as "unfit for human consumption" and often supplied as "research chemicals" or "plant food". There is no way of knowing what has gone into the production of these types of drugs and it's pretty foolish to take something with very little knowledge of what's in it or what effect it will have on your body

The Effects

It's impossible to say! Some of these products will mimic the effects of different drugs – Amphetamines, for instance, or cocaine. Others will give no effects whatsoever, other than a possible placebo effect of making the user *think* they're effected by the drug which may, in fact, contain nothing other than talcum powder and glucose.

Here's the danger – you don't really know what you're taking and you don't, therefore, know what the effects will be.

Legal Highs and Driving

Again, it's very difficult to judge when you don't know exactly what you've taken. Some of the stronger varieties will have effects such as euphoria, blurred vision, lack of inhibitions and poor co-ordination, which are very much incompatible with safe driving. Others might have no effect whatsoever.

If you're taking these drugs, there is an assumption that your *intention* is to get high, so whatever the actual effects of the drug are (or are not), you should avoid driving whilst you're taking them.

The Morning After

Again, the uncertainty of these types of drugs means that you need to be very careful to ensure you're no longer affected before you get back behind the wheel. To be as sure as you can be, my advice is to leave it 48 hours before driving if you've taken any kind of legal high – even if you don't think it's had any effect on you.

Nitrous Oxide

The other most common "legal" high is Nitrous Oxide, or "Laughing Gas". Nitrous Oxide is a gas with several legitimate uses, but it has become a commonly used recreational drug over the past few years.

One of the legitimate uses of Nitrous Oxide is as an aerosol gas used in the production of "whipped" cream. It is commercially available in small 3" canisters which are sold as "cream chargers" for whipped cream machines – they look like very small gas canisters.

Using a "cracker" which sits over the neck of the canister and breaks the seal, users generally use the gas to inflate a balloon before inhaling the gas from the balloon (when the gas comes straight out of the canister it is very cold and can cause burns, so decanting the gas into a balloon is safer).

The Effects

Nitrous Oxide brings on feelings of euphoria, relaxation and calmness. It also causes dizziness, difficulty in thinking straight and fits of giggles/laughter.
Some users also experience sound distortions and/or hallucinations.

Nitrous Oxide and Driving

The intoxicating effects of Nitrous Oxide as described above are not compatible with driving safely. If you're taking Nitrous Oxide, you should avoid driving immediately afterwards.

The Morning After

Having said all that, the effects of Nitrous Oxide wear off quite quickly. Many of you may have undergone dental procedures whilst sedated by Nitrous Oxide and even after having been rendered unconscious, you can be feeling normal again within a few hours.

To be on the safe side, if you've taken Nitrous Oxide – and *only* Nitrous Oxide – you should wait for 6 hours before driving again. If you've taken it with alcohol, or with other drugs, then you should wait considerably longer before driving.

Khat

Khat is a green, leafy plant which contains two types of stimulant drug. It is generally consumed by chewing the leaves of the plant and was recently classified as a class "C" controlled drug in the UK, so possessing or supplying Khat is now a criminal offence.

Khat originated in North Africa and Arabia and its consumption is most common amongst people who originate from these areas.

The Effects

The effects of Khat include alertness, arousal, a feeling of increased concentration, overconfidence, euphoria, hyperactivity, increased blood pressure, increased heart rate, insomnia, psychosis, a suppressed appetite and talkativeness.

Effects of long-term use can include depression, infrequent hallucinations, impaired inhibition (similar to alcohol), increased risk of heart attack and psychosis.

Khat and Driving

One of the problems with Khat is that users often take the drug for its stimulant properties, so that they can stay awake and alert whilst working long hours or driving long distances. Although users may feel as though they have more energy and that they are more alert, in fact, the other effects of the drug have a negative effect on their ability to drive and they're at a much increased risk of having an accident.

There is a much increased risk that users will make rash, badly-considered decisions after taking Khat and co-ordination and motor skills are also affected.

The Morning After

The immediate effects of Khat can last up to 6 hours, but the intoxicating effects are often followed by a significant "come down" which can also be debilitating and negatively affect your ability to drive safely.

If you use Khat, you should wait at least 24 hours after your last usage before driving again.

Poppers

Poppers, or Amyl Nitrite is a drug supplied in liquid form which is taken by sniffing the fumes directly from the bottle. It has traditionally been legal to possess and supply poppers in the UK, but the Imminent Psychoactive Substances Act will effectively make Poppers illegal in the UK.

The Effects

Amyl Nitrites dilate the blood vessels and allow more blood to get to the heart and brain. They give a "head rush" which lasts a few minutes and are reported to have a short-term effect on sexual experience.

Poppers and Driving

Although the effects of Poppers can be fairly short-term, these short-term effects are still incompatible with driving – dizziness, light-headedness, impulsiveness and lack of co-ordination are all effects which could easily lead to an individual making very bad decisions if they were driving a car, so driving after taking poppers it very much to be avoided.

Although you may feel fine again less than 15 minutes after taking poppers, there is one side effect which you should be acutely aware off – the possibility of "poppers maculopathy" This is a temporary or even permanent loss of vision, and if you experience this symptom, you should avoid driving completely and see your doctor as soon as possible.

The Morning After

The effects of poppers wear off quite quickly, so if you've taken poppers – and *only* poppers – you should be fine to drive again after waiting 6 hours.

Prescription Drugs

Researching the most common and popular recreational drugs was quite an undertaking and I'm aware that there are many less popular drugs that I've missed out. Researching the effects of every different prescription drug could take me years and I'd end up with a book much like a pharmacist's directory, so I'm not going to take that approach. Instead I'm going to keep this section brief and give you some very straightforward advice in relation to prescription drugs.

The difficulty with prescription drugs is that, firstly, some of them have intended effects which will help you with whatever your medical condition is, but at the same time, those positive effects (sleeping tablets for instance) are incompatible with safe driving.

Secondly, many drugs have side effects which may make it unsafe for you to drive. The added complication with side effects is that they can affect different people in different ways, so one person may take a drug and suffer no side effects whatsoever, and someone else may take exactly the same drug and suffer debilitating side effects.

The really important piece of advice is that, before taking any new prescription drug, or before changing your prescription, you should have a detailed conversation with your doctor about your prescription and how it will affect you and your ability to drive.

You shouldn't only be thinking about whether you'll be able to drive, of course – you should primarily be thinking about whether the drug is right for you, whether it will help your condition (surely this is the most important consideration?!), whether it could have any negative side effects and what to do if you experience them.

But part of that conversation has to be "will I still be safe to drive?"

Your doctor will give you a clear indication as to whether the new drugs will affect your ability to drive safely and it's important that you take their advice. It's also important, whenever you start a new prescription, to keep a close eye on yourself and how your body is reacting to the new drugs. If you're ever in any doubt, don't drive.

If you think your new prescription is affecting you in a way you're not happy with, go back to your doctor and discuss it with them.

If you look at the bigger picture, your health is always more important than your ability to drive (even if you drive for a living), and if your doctor recommends a course of drugs which would prevent you from driving, you should really bite the bullet, take the drugs and stop driving whilst you're on them.

Distraction in vehicle   3%

3% of all accidents and 6% of all fatal accidents are caused by distraction *inside* the vehicle. That's almost 3000 accidents and 84 people killed per year because of a distraction inside the vehicle – this is worth exploring in more detail.

It's easy to assume that everyone driving on the public roads is, at least, paying *some* attention to what they're doing, but as we've discussed elsewhere, many people aren't concentrating properly on their driving. They're giving *some* thought to the driving, but often the majority of their concentration is being taken up by thoughts about what will happen at work, what they're having for tea, what shoes to buy and whether or not to apply for that job they've seen advertised.

Now, this is ok to a point, but there are a number of distractions which can occur inside your car which could, if you let them, take up the small amount of concentration you're applying to your driving and – for a short time at least – take your concentration completely away from the fact that you're driving a car along a road at speed.

And this isn't a problem which is only experienced by inexperienced or inattentive drivers – very well trained and experienced drivers can also become distracted if they allow themselves to, and you only need to take your thoughts away from your driving for two or three seconds for things to go badly wrong.

Let's start with the biggest potential in-car distraction:

Passengers

Passengers are a constant distraction from driving – they want to talk to you whilst you're trying to drive, point out stuff in shop windows when you're trying to concentrate and ask you questions when you'd prefer to be thinking about what lane you need to be in at the next junction.

Then there are those passengers who like to fiddle with the heater controls and the radio – messing up your personal settings and your OCD about how your air vents are set (my Mum used to be terrible at this!).

If you're out in the evening, your passengers may be drunk and having a *much* better time than you! Drunk passengers can be terribly distracting and are one of the reasons I could never be a taxi driver.

So how do you prevent passengers from distracting you too much from your driving? It's a difficult balance – on the one hand you don't want them to feel completely ignored, but on the other hand, if you fully engage with them all the time whilst you're driving, you're likely to become excessively distracted at some points during your journey.

I have a couple of tactics I use, depending on the passengers...

"Hang on" is my favourite. If I'm approaching a multi-lane roundabout, trying to interpret the direction sign, pick the correct lane on approach and concentrate on whether I'll need to stop and give way, it's not the best time for Mrs Local to ask me "what did you think of The Walking Dead last night?"

As much as I'd like to discuss the latest episode of everyone's favourite zombie drama, at that point I'd prefer to keep my mind on my driving until I'm at least on to the roundabout and I know where I'm going, so I'll say "hang on". Mrs Local always takes the hint and it's only a few seconds before I've less to think about and I'm able to continue with both the journey and the conversation about killing the undead hoards.

Shall we get a takeaway? "Hang on".

I'm looking forward to our holiday this year. "Hang on".

What would you do if you slipped off a ledge and were left dangling by your fingers? "Hang on".

You get the idea – you're not being rude – just asking them to pause the conversation for a few seconds until you've a little extra spare mental capacity to engage with them.

Having an argument in the car, on the other hand, is a little more difficult to manage. The other participant has you at a disadvantage, because you're unable to give your full attention to the argument and if you do, there is a very real possibility that you'll be dangerously distracted.

If you're having a row, it's always best to pull over and stop somewhere safe so that you can argue without the danger of having an accident.

Drunk passengers can be a pain but, whenever possible, I ask them to sit in the back seats. Drunks in the rear are far less able to distract you (and a little easier to ignore) than when they're sat in the front – right next to you.

Children

Children bring with them a world of distraction! Anyone who has ever travelled any distance with children of any age will tell you that they can be very difficult to manage, even on the shortest journeys.

There is no secret to dealing with this distraction – the solutions involve planning ahead, knowing what your children enjoy (and what keeps them quiet), and having a couple of tactics to prevent them becoming excessively distracting.

Firstly, sit them in the back. Most car seats are safer when fitted in the rear seats anyway, but children in the back seat are less distracting than those sat in the front.

Secondly, try to keep *them* distracted. Give them something to do, or something to occupy them during your journey. These days, tablet computers or game consoles are good, even for younger children, but sometimes there's nothing better than a game of "I-Spy" or "Yellow" (trying to be the first to spot a yellow car) to keep kids amused. If they're happily playing a game or spotting things, they're far less likely to behave in a way which distracts you from driving.

Plan your journey so that you're not caught out with a small child needing the loo. Make sure they go before you set off and try to stop at least every hour on a long journey to give them the chance to use the toilet.

Many children find riding in a car very relaxing and will fall asleep shortly after setting off. Make the most of it! Practising a smooth driving style will help the little darlings nod off quickly and allow you to keep your concentration to a maximum.

Animals

Animals have an air of unpredictability about them which concerns me. You wouldn't travel with an unrestrained hyperactive child in the car would you? Or allow a young child to travel with their head out of the window? But many people seem happy to allow their beloved dogs to travel like this, despite the dangers it can pose.

The best advice if you travel with a dog in the car (or a cat, or ferrets, or llamas – I'm not judging), is to keep the animal in a secure area within the car, away from the driver. Rear hatch or estate car boots with a dividing dog barrier are good, as are cages which can be kept within the car, on the passenger seat etc. If you introduce your dog to the concept of travelling within a cage inside the car at an early age, they'll easily adapt to it and the dog will be safer in the event of an accident.

If you absolutely must travel with your dog on a passenger seat, you can buy a harness which clicks into the cars seatbelt and keeps the dog under control, and restrained in the event of an accident.

Smoking

Many people like to smoke and it's not yet become a criminal offence to smoke whilst you're driving (unless you've got children in the car with you, in which case, in England and Wales, it *is* now a criminal offence).

Now, although I've always been a non-smoker, I'm not really one to judge, and if you like to smoke in the car it's fine with me, but just be aware that smoking can be an unnecessary distraction from your driving.

If you're opening a cigarette packet or getting one out to light it, try to do it when your car is stationary. If you must do it on the move, do it when you're on a straight stretch of road with few hazards, so that you don't end up opening a packet & lighting up whilst steering with your knees and changing gear with your elbow.

One of the things smokers will tell you is that there is nothing worse than dropping a lit cigarette in the car whilst you're driving. You'll finish your fag, open the window to drop it out and a gust of wind will blow it back into the car – under your seat if you're lucky or onto your lap if you're unlucky.

I can't imagine anything much more distracting than having a red-hot fag end landing in your lap and burning through your trouser leg whilst you're driving along the motorway at 70mph!

This is one of the reasons you should never throw your cigarette ends out of your car window. The others are that they can be a hazard to motorcyclists (they really don't like getting a face full of cigarette butt at high speed), and the simple fact that it's dirty and anti-social.

Instead, use your ashtray – it's much safer, less anti-social and you're far less likely to end up in a ball of flames on the hard shoulder!

Eating and Drinking

Yes, we've all read the stories about someone who has been prosecuted by an overzealous police officer for eating a banana in stationary traffic, or sipping from a can of coke whilst stopped at traffic lights, but how much of a distraction *is* eating or drinking at the wheel?

I'm not so sure that *just* eating or *just* drinking are particularly distracting. I think it's more the other associated actions which can be a distraction – opening a sandwich packet, peeling a banana, opening some crisps or cracking open a can of pop. These action are the things which can – and do – cause unnecessary distractions to drivers and can cause accidents.

So my advice is to prepare the food for eating or the drink for drinking whilst you're stationary and make sure that whatever you're consuming isn't getting in the way of your driving. If you think it is, pull over and finish your meal before setting off again.

Driver/Rider illness or disability, mental or physical
2%

Over 2400 accidents occur every year due to a driver becoming physically or mentally ill, or because of a disability.

It would be very easy to dismiss these types of accident as "just one of those things". After all, if someone falls ill at the wheel, it's not really their fault is it? They didn't *mean* to collapse at the wheel did they? They just fell ill. It's just one of those things.

Isn't it?

Well, to be brutally honest, in most cases, no, it isn't. I dealt with a number of accidents – including a couple of fatal accidents – whilst I was in the police, which were primarily caused by a driver falling ill whilst they were driving. In every single case, those drivers were either fully aware that they were suffering from the medical condition which caused the accident, or had recently suffered symptoms which would have indicated that they were suffering from the condition which caused the accident.

If those individuals had either followed their doctor's advice, or allowed themselves to be examined by a doctor when they first experienced symptoms, none of those accidents – including the fatal ones – would have occurred.

This book is primarily about how you can prevent being involved in an accident, and my intention was to write about driving and how to drive in a way that should help you avoid having an accident. However, as I've looked at contributory factors in more detail, it seems that some of them involve much more than just driving issues, and actually become general advice about how to live your life, how to organise yourself and how to take responsibility for your own actions. So at the risk of sounding like one of those bloody awful American "life coaches", I'll cover the points I want to make.

Let's look at the basics. There are certain attributes that you absolutely must be in possession of if you want to drive a motor vehicle. You need to be able to see clearly (and we'll look at eyesight later in this chapter), you need to be able to physically maintain control of a car, you need to be able to think rationally and make sensible decisions, and you need to be able to remain conscious.

Those are the basics.

If, at any time, you are in doubt about your ability in any of those areas, you should see your doctor as soon as possible. If you're being responsible, you should also stop driving until you've seen your doctor and had a diagnosis. You should also discuss with your doctor whether or not you should continue driving whilst your condition is being either diagnosed or treated.

Here's the important bit – if your doctor advises you to stop driving for the time being, you *must* stop driving. You may feel fine, you may think it's something of nothing and you may think that stopping driving will be a major inconvenience to you.

But believe me – collapsing unconscious at the wheel and killing a number of innocent pedestrians is far more of an inconvenience to yourself and everyone else than just following some straightforward medical advice. Ask the Glasgow bin lorry driver who collapsed at the wheel in 2010. Here was a man who had deliberately concealed a medical condition for 40 years, knowing full well that it could, at any time, render him unconscious.

He didn't mean to hurt anybody, of course, and his intentions in concealing his medical condition were simply to allow him to continue working and earning a living.

But on that day in 2010, he fell unconscious at the wheel of his 32-ton lorry, which then ploughed into a crowd of pedestrians in a busy city centre, killing 6 and seriously injuring 15 others.

This, of course, is at the extreme end of the spectrum, but I have personally dealt with two fatal accidents which could easily have been prevented if the drivers involved had either sought medical advice when they experienced some pretty obvious symptoms, or actually followed their doctor's advice to stop driving.

Self-Awareness

There are many medical conditions which, with a sensible attitude and appropriate medication, can easily be managed and which need not prevent you from driving. Diabetes is a good example. There are various levels of type 2 diabetes, ranging from those who simply manage the condition with diet and exercise, through those who take medication and up to those who are insulin-dependent.

None of these levels of diabetes should prevent anyone from driving, but the key point in dealing with diabetes is that you need to be aware of the condition and its possible effects. The first stage in any treatment for diabetes is to make the individual aware of the condition and what it's effects are.

On more than one occasion, I've found diabetic patients unconscious behind the wheel of their car after suffering a hypoglycaemic attack. I've pursued a diabetic driver for several miles thinking that he was extremely drunk when, in fact, he was suffering a hypo. I've even had to inform a family that their father had died in an accident because he blacked out and crashed into a tree because he hadn't managed his blood sugar levels properly that day.

These people were all aware that they were diabetic, and they all had a reasonable awareness of their condition, but on these particular days, they failed to manage their condition properly. That's bad enough if you're at home or pottering in the garden, but if you're driving round at speed in a ton-and-a-half of car, you're potentially putting other people's lives at risk and in my book that is completely unacceptable.

I've used diabetes as an example because it's a fairly common and well-known medical condition, but my point is valid for any other medical condition – heart conditions, mental health problems, conditions of the nervous system, physical injuries which restrict your ability to operate the cars controls and any one of a thousand other medical problems.

Please – be honest with yourself and take any advice you're given by a doctor. It's not just your life you're risking – it's everyone else's around you too.

What if someone close to you has a condition which makes driving risky, but they continue to drive?

This is one of those moral dilemmas that we could all face at some point – do you allow them to carry on driving because, well, you know, it's their independence and it keeps them going and they'd just deteriorate if they couldn't get out and about...

Or do you take the wider view that allowing them to continue driving puts everyone else on the road at risk and you wouldn't want an accident on your conscience, would you?

It's a difficult choice, and one many people struggle with, but if you'd ever suffered the loss of a loved one in a road accident, I don't think you'd really struggle very hard with the decision.

If you suspect someone shouldn't be driving because of a medical condition, or just because you think they're getting too old and infirm to drive safely, you should do something about it.

Talk to them first if you can. Sometimes people actually *want* the inevitable pointing out to them – it may come as a relief for someone to point out that their driving is getting worse and it's quite common – more common than you think – for people to happily give up driving when it's suggested by a close friend or relative.

If they're not minded to give up voluntarily, it might be worth having a word with their GP. Doctors aren't legally obliged to report medically unfit drivers to the DVSA, but there is a system where they can report such drivers if they think they are a danger to others.

As a last resort, you can report these matters to the police. Police officers just want to prevent accidents and will be happy to pay someone a visit to discuss and advise them on whether they are still fit to drive or not. It doesn't have to lead to a prosecution, or to any kind of formal action, but sometimes a chat with a police officer can be enough to persuade someone to stop driving.

I appreciate that this is a difficult subject, but it's one that many of us will have to deal with at some time.

Fatigue   2%

2% of all accidents are attributed to driver fatigue, but fatigue actually accounts for 3% of all fatal accidents.

Some academic studies have concluded that fatigue is just as debilitating – and just as impairing – as alcohol and have compared driving whilst tired very closely with driving whilst drunk.

We've all been tired, and I'm sure that almost all of us have driven when we've been tired too – after an unexpectedly long shift at work, after a night out or on a particularly long journey. Part of the problem is that fatigue creeps up on us – we're not deliberately tired and we might not feel tired at the start of our journey, but, over time, tiredness slowly creeps up on us, wraps its arms around us like a nice, warm blanket and starts to take effect.

You'll start to experience difficulty in focusing, and a narrowing of your field of vision. Your reaction times are increased and your judgement becomes impaired. You start to "zone out", your thoughts start to wander and you become susceptible to daydreaming. You'll drift within your lane and start to experience that feeling where you cannot remember the last few minutes of your journey. Eventually, you'll actually start to nod off for very short – but, crucially – very dangerous periods of time.

The Causes

There are two main causes of driver fatigue:

Lack of sleep, and;

Driving at times when you'd normally be sleeping.

Our bodies need sleep. I've spoken to people who claim to be able to function without or with very little sleep, but the truth is that we all require a decent amount of sleep every day in order to allow us to continue functioning normally.

I'm not an expert on sleep, and there are various opinions about how much sleep we all need – opinions seem to vary considerably and seem to be dependent on a number of factors such as your sex, age, weight, level of physical activity and so on.

The key is that if you *don't* get enough sleep, or if your sleep is of a poor quality, you'll be susceptible to fatigue if you need to drive anywhere – particularly over a long distance. It's important, then, that if you're planning a long car journey, you should make sure you get enough sleep beforehand.

I worked unsocial shifts for nearly 20 years, so I'm reasonably well qualified to comment on driving at times when you'd normally be sleeping. Our bodies have evolved to sleep at night, when it's dark and quiet, and to be awake during the day when it's light and busy.

If you take your body out of that pattern, it can respond in a very negative way. Working unsocial shifts moves your body clock around and forces your body to be active when it should be resting and vice-versa.

There is, however, no way of avoiding shift working if you choose certain professions and the most important thing to bear in mind if you have to drive at unusual hours of the day or night is this:

You Should Monitor Your Own Levels of Fatigue

This isn't easy – it requires you to be honest with yourself about how you're feeling (something we're not very good at), and to do something about it if you think you are fatigued.

If you're driving and you start to experience any of the symptoms I've listed above, you should stop as soon as it's safe to do so and take a break. You might want to get out of the car and have a walk around to wake yourself up – this is fine if you haven't got much further to travel – say another half-an-hour or so.

If you need to travel for longer than half-an-hour, my advice is to stop and rest in your car. Have a nap – even a short 15 or 30-minute nap can rebalance your "sleep debt" enough to allow you to continue safely with your journey.

Some people like to take caffeine in either a hot drink or an energy drink when they're tired. Caffeine is s mild stimulant drug and, in the short term, can help you fight the effects of fatigue and feel less tired. If you stop when you feel tired and drink a strong coffee or an energy drink, the caffeine will start to have an effect almost immediately and will peak after 30-60 minutes. The effect will start to slowly wear off and will have effectively stopped after 2 or 3 hours.

This is ok in the short term, but if you start to rely on caffeine in the longer term, you may make things works. Caffeine will prevent you from sleeping, and if you're taking something which prevents you from sleeping to combat a problem which is actually *caused* by lack of sleep, you'll cause yourself some serious problems.

Drivers of heavy goods vehicles and large passenger carrying vehicles are legally obliged to take regular breaks and days off from driving. This is to ensure that fatigue doesn't affect these drivers and cause them to have accidents.

Take a leaf from their book. Get plenty of rest and if you start to feel tired, take a break as soon as possible.

Distraction outside vehicle   2%

We looked at distraction inside the vehicle earlier in this chapter, so it's only right that we consider distractions *outside* the vehicle as well, as this contributory factor accounts for over 1500 accidents a year.

In the first chapter I looked at how you can improve your concentration skills and how to look down the road and around your vehicle to take in everything you need to make your next driving plans. What I didn't mention is the stuff you *don't* need to be looking at – the irrelevant stuff which distracts you from the act of actually *driving* and prevents you from concentrating and planning properly.

You all know the stuff I'm talking about – those lovely shoes in that shop window, that new Porsche on the garage forecourt, the dolly bird in the *very* tight shorts* and the lovely, fluffy new lambs in that field over there.

*And whatever the male equivalent is – I'm not discriminating!

There is, of course, nothing wrong with looking at these things, but you need to make sure they're not distracting you too much from the fact that you're driving a moving car. So if you absolutely *must* look at the shoes/Porsche/shorts/lambs, you should do so in the same way that you look at everything else when you're driving – quick glances. Don't stare at anything for too long, because if you do, you'll have travelled some distance towards everything else that you're *not* looking at!

Keep scanning, in other words, or keep colouring in. Look at the irrelevant stuff by all means, but please keep looking at everything else too! You're not a passenger – passengers can gawp freely at anything they want to for as long as they like without fear of crashing.

Rider wearing dark clothing   0% (578)

This accounts for a small number of accidents and I think it's better if I combine this contributory factor with the next one:

Not displaying lights at night or in poor visibility 0% (431)

In excess of 1000 accidents a year are caused by drivers not displaying lights at night or in poor visibility, or by riders ("riders are not further defined, so we'll presume any kinds of riders – cyclists, motorcyclists, horse riders, pogo sick riders and emu jockeys) wearing dark clothing.

Let's start with the dark clothing issue. Riders, if you're out on the road at night, or even during the day, do you prefer other drivers to be able to see you or not?

What? You'd prefer them to see you? Yes, I can appreciate your point of view – probably better that the drivers of large, fast-moving lumps of metal are able to see you and avoid you.

DON'T WEAR DARK CLOTHING THEN!

Come on guys and girls, this isn't rocket science – if you wear dark clothing, particularly at night, but also during the day, you're making yourself far less visible than if you choose to wear something bright & high-vis. I know high-vis isn't really very fashionable, but I'd rather be alive in flared jeans than dead in a designer jacket, wouldn't you?

In all seriousness, riders of any description should take some responsibility and wear something bright to make themselves as easily visible as possible, but – and this is the bit that the car drivers need to take heed of – sometimes they don't!

Sometimes they like to wear dark clothing so that they blend seamlessly into the background. Sometimes they even like to add to the thrill by not using lights at night – sometimes even on unlit roads!

These people are out there, and we've all got a collective responsibility to look out for these idiots and to try not to kill them. So let's look at the use of headlights and how you can do everything possible to avoid hitting one of these "ghost" riders – or anything else, come to think of it...

There's nothing inherently dangerous or excessively risky about driving at night. We're lucky to live in a highly developed country with a relatively high proportion of well-lit roads, particularly in urban and suburban areas.

Having said that, there are still many thousands of miles of unlit roads in between our towns and cities, but most modern cars have excellent lights and our annual MOT tests mean that most cars have defective bulbs replaced once a year at a minimum.

We also have many laws and regulations which govern what lights can or cannot be fitted to vehicles, how they must be maintained, and even when they must be switched on and off.

I know this doesn't sound particularly advanced, but next time you're abroad - even in countries which are considered as advanced as ours - try driving at night and you'll immediately notice the difference - both in the quality and quantity of street lighting, and in the maintenance and use of headlights.

At the risk of sounding like I'm teaching you to suck eggs, there are two key things to remember when driving at night...

(1) Its more difficult to see.

(2) Its more difficult for others to see you.

Although having said that, there are a couple of advantages to visibility at night which we'll look at in a bit.

To help with both of these issues, car manufacturers fit a variety of different lights to their cars, so we'll start with a brief look at the legalities of driving at night.

Drivers **must** use **sidelights** between **sunset and sunrise.**

Additionally, drivers must use **(dipped) headlights** during the **hours of darkness (half-an-hour after sunset until half-an-hour before sunrise),** *except* when using a road which has lit street lighting, in which case the only *legal* requirement is to use sidelights.

It's also a legal requirement to use **headlights** when visibility is seriously reduced (generally when, due to weather conditions or perhaps smoke, visibility is reduced to less than 100 metres).

Note that there is no legal requirement to use foglights when visibility is seriously reduced. The legislation outlines when you should *not* use foglights, but there is no law which states that you *have* to use them.

There is a lot more to the legislation, but for most car drivers, that's all you need to know.

Although the legislation only requires sidelights at night in built-up areas, bearing in mind item (2) above, I can see no logical reason why you would not choose to use dipped beam headlights at all times when it's dark. Even on an older car with weaker headlights, dipped beam lights make your vehicle much more visible to other road users, so my advice is to use dipped beam headlights at all times when you're driving at night and save the sidelights for parking.

One thing to be careful of here - some car manufacturers, Vauxhall for instance, have an annoying habit of designing cars with instrument binnacles which light up night and day when the ignition is switched on, irrespective of whether the lights are switched on or not. It's very easy, particularly if you're in a well-lit area at night, to get in one of these cars, see the dashboard light up, assume the lights are on and drive off into the gloom, wondering why everyone is flashing at you. I did it myself a few times when the police panda fleet was updated about 10 years ago. You're less likely to do it if your own car has this feature, because we all tend to know our own cars well, but always look for the green symbol on the dash to confirm your lights are on.

So, built-up areas, street lights etc. - there's not a lot to say really. Leave your headlights on dipped beam, position yourself generally towards the centre of the road to allow vehicles approaching junctions to your left to get a slightly earlier view of you and try to go handbrake-neutral when you're stationary as modern brake lights can be very dazzling to drivers behind.

Many vehicles these days - my own included - are fitted with automatic headlights. Just flick the light switch to the "A" setting and the car monitors how light or dark it is and switches the lights on and off as appropriate. They are generally good systems and I use mine, but there are a couple of things to bear in mind.

Firstly, they will come on during the day if you enter a tunnel. This is generally a good thing, but can be misinterpreted by other drivers as a headlight flash, so keep a careful eye on the drivers around you and expect the occasional lane change.

Secondly, be careful if you lend your car to someone else, or if it goes in for service. It's easy to take automatic lights for granted (mine never move from the "A" position), and then be caught out if someone else uses your car and switches them off.

A note on courtesy. It seems to be a well-established tradition in this country that drivers acknowledge a courtesy by flashing their headlights. Personally, I can't think of a worse way to thank someone than by burning their retinas out and leaving them temporarily partially blinded. You wouldn't thank someone for buying you a pint by poking them in the eyes, would you?

I know a "thank you" wave isn't really visible at night, so my preference is to momentarily turn my lights from dipped-beam to sidelights and then back to dipped-beam again. It will acknowledge a courtesy from an oncoming driver without causing them to drive into the nearest bus shelter.

On unlit rural roads, there is much more to think about when it comes to lighting. The priority moves from being seen, to being able to see, and this is where you need to make use - by which I mean *intelligent* use - of your "main", "high" or "full" beam headlights.

If you are on an unlit road and there are no vehicles in front, use your main beam. It will illuminate the road much further ahead and allow a planned approach to hazards. It will also give you the best chance of seeing those pesky unlit riders in their dark clothing and invisibility cloaks!

If you can see the headlights or tail lights of a car ahead, you should switch your lights to dipped beam. The principle is that if you can see their lights, they can see yours and you really don't want to dazzle the driver of a vehicle which is travelling towards you at speed.

There is usually no need to dip your lights *before* you see headlights or tail lights. Many people dip their lights when they see the "halo" of oncoming vehicles but this isn't usually necessary.

The exception with this point is for large goods vehicles with a raised driving position. These vehicles have headlights fitted at normal height but the driver sits higher up, so it is possible to dazzle them even if you can't see their headlights, so dip early if you think it's an HGV approaching.

If I'm on an unlit road at night, using main beam, I don't generally dip my lights if I see a vehicle approaching a junction to the left or right. Over the years, I have found that dipping lights under these circumstances can be misunderstood by the vehicles in the junction as a signal to pull out. People are much less likely to pull out in front of a vehicle with high beam displayed than one which has just dipped its lights. You won't find this in a textbook anywhere - it's just based on my own observations. It might seem a little inconsiderate to dazzle a car in a junction, but they can look away safely and you can also usually pick out the driver and observe their actions better if your lights remain on high beam. If the vehicle pulls out regardless then, of course, dip your lights.

When overtaking, keep your lights on dipped beam until the front of your car has passed the door mirrors of the overtaken car - or the front most overtaken car if you're overtaking multiple vehicles.

If you are being overtaken, or you think the car behind wants to overtake, help them out by keeping your main beam on until their door mirrors have passed the front of your car, and then dip your lights.

The "halo" I mentioned earlier is one of the biggest advantages of driving at night. During the day, your view is limited by hedges, trees, buildings etc. but at night, the halo of headlights can give you a very clear indication as to which direction the road is going and how severe the corners ahead are.

And one final reminder – there are some invisible ghost riders out there. Keep them in mind and keep your eyes peeled – you'll spot them early one day and you'll thank Reg for the advice (I know it should be them thanking me, but we've already established that they're idiots!).

Driver using mobile phone   0% (492)

Of all the statistics I examined whilst researching this book, I think this one was by far the most surprising. I've asked a number of people what percentage of accidents are caused by drivers using mobile phones and the answers have ranged from

25% up to 80%. The most common figure is somewhere between 40% and 50%.

I was a little more conservative – I'd have put the figure somewhere between 15% and 20% before I started my research.

Imagine how surprised I was to find out that in 2014, only 0.43% of all accidents were attributed to a driver using their mobile phone.

0.43%! That's just 492 out of over 115,000 accidents nationally.

If you were to believe the press (you should never believe the press, by the way, but that's another story), the Government (same principle), road safety campaigners and the police (ahem), using a mobile phone whilst driving is causing hundreds and thousands of deaths and injuries on our roads every day. You can hardly walk out of your house for fear of being struck and wounded by a maniac who is driving whilst chatting on his phone.

In fact, in 2014, more accidents were caused by emergency vehicles on a call (578), Riders wearing dark clothing (578) and vehicle door opened or closed negligently (656), than by people using their mobile phones whilst driving.

Clearly, however, the statistics do not support the hype about driving & using the phone. I think there's one main reason for this, and it's the same reason that accident statistics for speeding motorists are also surprisingly low…

People lie.

I don't mean it in a nasty way, but if you were involved in an accident because you were texting or updating your Facebook status on your phone, would you admit it to the police when they arrived?

No – I thought not. It may be clear that you are responsible for the accident, that you lost control or were distracted, and that may not be something that you can easily deny, but when asked if you were using your phone – like most other people – you'll lie.

I'm not making any judgements here, by the way – just sharing my long experience of human nature, particularly after an accident.

"How did the accident happen Sir?"

"I was driving along when a black dog ran out in front of me and I crashed into all those stationary cars, Officer"

"I see Sir – and were you speeding?"

"No, officer – I was doing 25mph".

"And were you using your phone at the time?"

"No Officer – definitely not".

The problem is, if the accident was minor in nature (most are), the police won't have the time or resources to seize and examine your phone to prove whether or not you were using it at the time, so in the absence of any other evidence, they won't tick the box which suggests that you were on the phone.

In reality, I think that somewhere between 5% and 10% of accidents are caused in some part by inappropriate use of a mobile phone, which *is* a significant amount and is worth discussing.

Anything which takes your attention away from the thoughts and actions involved in driving a car adds to the risk that you'll have an accident. Calling someone on a hands-free phone brings with it a certain level of distraction and should really be avoided if at all possible. Calling someone on a hand-held phone is more distracting and can- and has - led to many serous and fatal accidents.

By far the most distracting and dangerous thing you can do with your mobile phone, however, is anything text-based, by which I mean SMS texting, emailing, Whatsapping, iMessaging, Tweeting, Facebook updating and any number of other activities which involve reading and writing text on your phone.

Now, in all honesty, this doesn't take a genius (or someone who claims to be an "expert" driver) to work out. It's obvious to anyone with half a brain that if you continually take your eyes off the road to read and write messages on your phone, you'll be excessively distracted from driving and putting yourself and others at serious risk of having an accident.

I thought about including loads of information about academic studies showing that texting is riskier than drink driving, how your reaction times are affected etc. But in the end I thought it was better to keep this as simple as possible.

If you're driving, put your phone out of reach.

Putting your phone out of reach – in your handbag, on the back seat, in your coat pocket on the back seat, in the boot etc. completely removes any temptation to ring people, answer calls, read and reply to texts and everything else you want to do on your phone.

Driving and using your mobile phone are two incompatible activities, so keep them separate! Keep your phone out of reach when you're driving. That way, if you absolutely *must* use the phone, you'll have to do the only safe thing you should do – pull over and stop.

Some cars have Bluetooth hands-free systems fitted as standard which automatically link to your phone every time you switch the ignition on. If you're an experienced driver and you don't think a conversation will distract you too much from driving, then you're probably ok to receive the occasional short call on hands-free. If you're inexperienced, however, or if you find conversations excessively distracting, just switch the Bluetooth off and leave the phone calls until you've stopped.

Other Drivers

There are loads of drivers out there using their phones, and they're easy to spot if you look for them. You'll still see plenty who are driving with their phone jammed up to their ear, of course, but have a look around you the next time you're stopped at traffic lights. Look how many drivers are constantly looking down into their laps. Are they really that interested in their own upper thighs?

No – of course not – they're all checking their phones for messages.

Have you ever been behind someone at some traffic lights which have turned to green, but the driver in front has stayed put – usually with their foot firmly on the brake pedal?

They're looking at their phone. Watch them jump when you give them a quick toot!

Texting drivers often weave and wander down the road in the same way that a drunk or drugged driver will. Small steering corrections every time they deem to look up from their phone for a quick glance, then back down to their phone again.

There are loads of these people out there. If you spot them, give them a wide birth – keep away from them so that if they are distracted to the point where they have an accident, that accident doesn't include you!

And it won't *be* you on the phone, will it? Because your phone will be out of reach!

Uncorrected, defective eyesight   0% (260)

I think this is another underreported contributory factor, by which I mean that there are probably many thousands of drivers out there with poor, uncorrected eyesight.

The minimum eyesight requirement in the UK requires you to be able to read a standard British number plate (with or without glasses or corrective lenses) at a distance of 20.5 metres – approximately 5 car lengths.

To be honest, this is a pretty low standard. I've worn glasses for short-sightedness since my late 20's and my prescription is fairly strong, but I can easily reach the minimum eyesight standard *without* wearing my glasses. I really wouldn't feel safe driving without glasses, but I'd be legally allowed to do so. Which is a worry.

I attended an accident one Sunday afternoon a few years ago – a lady in her 80's had failed to give way at a "T" junction and collided with a cyclist, causing a serious leg injury. It was a bright, clear day and the cyclist was wearing plenty of high-vis clothing. The junction had good views in both directions and there was no good reason for the lady to have failed to see the cyclist.

I decided to carry out an eyesight test, so I walked the lady 20 paces down the road from the scene, turned her around, and asked her to read out the number plate of my police car – my fully liveried police car which with flashing blue roof light.

"Which one is the police car?" she asked.

After some lengthy discussions with her family, she eventually agreed to surrender her driving licence.

One of the difficulties with poor eyesight is that, for the majority of people, the deterioration develops over a very long period of time. It's like children growing up – if you see them every day, you don't notice how much they've grown until someone who hasn't seen them for a couple of years points it out to you.

Deteriorating eyesight is something which happens naturally with age. If you haven't got any eyesight problems by the time you reach 30, you'll probably be fine until your mid-40's, but if you're a driver, it's always worth having an eyesight check every couple of years, irrespective of your age, even if you think your vision is fine.

Many opticians offer free eyesight tests these days – book yourself in and have your vision checked.

If you already wear glasses or contact lenses, you should keep up your opticians' appointments and have your vision checked at least every couple of years. Eyesight can continue to deteriorate and you should always make sure that your current prescription is up-to-date.

6. PEDESTRIAN ONLY (CASUALTY OR UNINJURED) (12% OF ALL ACCIDENTS)

Pedestrian failed to look properly   9%

Pedestrian careless, reckless or in a hurry   5%

Pedestrian failed to judge vehicle path or speed 3%

Crossing road masked by stationary or parked vehicle   2%

Pedestrian impaired by alcohol   2%

Pedestrian wrong use of pedestrian crossing facility 1%

Dangerous action in carriageway (e.g. playing) 1%

Pedestrian wearing dark clothing at night 1%

Pedestrian disability or illness, mental or physical 0% (498)

Pedestrian impaired by drugs (illicit or medicinal) 0% (210)

Of all road users, I think pedestrians worry me the most. There is no less predictable group of people on the roads, and none that are more vulnerable. Look at the long list of contributory factors above which has been drafted to account for all the daft, careless, inattentive and careless actions that pedestrians can be guilty of.

I should also add that a pedestrian accident is always a horrible experience for all involved and having witnessed one first hand myself, they are another experience to be completely avoided. These type of accidents definitely fall into the category where, even if, as a driver, you're completely innocent, the experience will live with you – and haunt you - for the rest of your life.

A big part of the problem is that pedestrians are so vulnerable. Sat in your car, surrounded by a ton-and-a-half of metal, seatbelts and airbags, you're pretty well protected in the event of a collision. Even motorcyclists and cyclists have some level of protection with leathers, gloves & helmets providing at least *some* protection.

But pedestrians aren't. And a pedestrian struck by a car at anything faster than 5-10mph is likely to suffer some level of serious injury. A pedestrian struck at an impact speed of anything more than about 20mph is very likely to die from their injuries.

Pedestrian accidents are also a very personal, intimate experience for those involved. Crash into a car or bus and you're just crashing into a machine – there may be individuals inside them – but you don't see them during the accident – just the vehicle.

But collide with a pedestrian and you see the person – the individual – as they interact, in the worst possible way, with your car. Many drivers who have struck pedestrians remember seeing their face as they strike them and the way their bodies react to the impact.

As I mentioned above, these accidents are horrible, and as a driver you're responsible for doing everything that you can to avoid pedestrian accidents. So where do we start? With the obvious? Don't drive on the pavement!

But if we're going to examine pedestrian accidents (and how to avoid them) in a little more detail, let's take a look at the weakest link in the chain – the pedestrians themselves.

What to look for?

When you're driving along, surrounded by other vehicles, it's safe to assume that *most* of the other drivers around you have a certain level of competence. They may not all be expert "Stig" level drivers, but most of them will at least have passed a driving test to prove a basic level of competence.

The incompetent drivers are required to display a sign which allows other road users to easily identify them.

It says "Taxi".

Only joking! I love taxi drivers really & they get an unnecessarily bad press. I do, of course, mean "L" plates. – they let us identify which drivers are not yet competent and may carry out unpredictable manoeuvres.

It's even reasonably easy to spot whether a cyclist is competent or not – are they wobbling in their lane or are they steady? Are they carrying out shoulder checks? Giving hand signals? The incompetent are fairly easy to spot and give a wide birth.

But pedestrians are different. You don't need a licence to be a pedestrian. You don't need to pass a walking test, or obtain foot tax or shoe insurance. It's perfectly legal to walk along the road whilst drunk or mentally ill. There are no eyesight requirements or other health restrictions on pedestrians. You just need to be able to walk. Or run. Or stagger.

Out of the large number of pedestrians you encounter during a typical journey, can you easily pick out and identify which of them is drunk? Or on drugs? Or deaf? Have a look at how many are staring intently at their phones as they negotiate busy traffic on foot. And at how many are wearing earphones.

Pedestrians have different priorities than other road users. They're intently interested in SMSs, Facebook and twitter. They listen to music through their headphones to drown out the traffic noise and they're not usually giving much attention to their journey – they're walking to get somewhere and that is where their mind will be.

There are times when pedestrians are *more* likely to act carelessly. Rain can be a particular problem - most people would seemingly prefer to risk an impact with a moving vehicle than get slightly wet. Umbrellas also remove most of their field of vision and make them even more likely to leap out in front of you.

When it's raining, people are rushing more and are likely to make quick, ill-considered decisions about when they should cross the road. If they've got their hoods up, they'll have much reduced peripheral vision and if they're thinking of crossing the road, they won't have a full view of traffic from a quick glance backwards, so look out for hoods, headscarves, burkas or any other items of clothing which reduces pedestrians' field of vision.

We all know that unaccompanied children can be a problem, but even if children are accompanied by adults, there is nothing to say that the adults aren't idiots! Look to see whether they're holding the child's hand or whether they're running free.

There also seems to be a particularly strange habit amongst some mothers of "testing" the traffic with a child's buggy before crossing the road. I see this quite often – the mother with a child in a buggy will stop, turn to face the road and then stick the front of the pram out into the traffic in much the same way as they might test the temperature of a bath with their elbow. It's almost as though they're happy to sacrifice their child to ensure they can cross safely! It's the modern equivalent of the old miner's canary!

I'm very wary of people walking dogs. Always look to see if the dog is under control and on a leash. If it's not, it may well act unpredictably. This can often lead to other vehicles swerving to avoid the dog or the dog owner running into the road after the dog and becoming a casualty themselves.

Alcohol has a strange effect on some people – particularly young men. It makes them think they are completely invincible to cars and buses and gives them the ability to randomly step into the road – often in groups (they're even more invincible in groups) – in front of all manner of traffic travelling at all manner of speeds.

This type of behaviour is, of course, much more likely late at night and in busy town centres at weekends, so if you're out driving at those times, be prepared for people to step out unexpectedly and adjust your speed and position so that you can avoid them if they do.

And if you think I'm exaggerating, I promise you I'm not. I used to drive a police car regularly on emergency response runs and even when I was on "blues and twos", it was very common for pedestrians to unexpectedly step out in front of me. If they'll do it to a police car with two tone sirens, flashing blue lights and headlights, they'll do it to you.

A couple of more specific scenarios to bar in mind. Firstly, lines of parked cars.

It's very easy for children to cross suddenly from in between lines of parked cars at the side of the road. They can be well hidden, and can also be travelling quite quickly when they emerge, suddenly, in front of your car.

Practice looking to the left and right of parked cars – on the pavements and even into driveways and pathways to the left and right of the road. You may well spot some movement early which could end up being a child about to run out. When a good driver is driving past lines of parked cars, they'll look almost as though they're watching a tennis match – their heads constantly moving from left to right, scanning to the sides looking for movements.

Additionally, look *underneath* the parked cars as you approach them. You can't see through the vehicles, but you can see the movement of feet and this can be an invaluable observation link.

Remember this too – children usually travel around in packs. So if one child runs out – or cycles out – in front of you, there is a strong likelihood that more will do the same. Don't just avoid the one who runs out – think about the others who may follow.

The other specific scenario is buses. Or to be more precise, people crossing the road in front of buses.

This is a little more personal to me as I dealt with two particularly distressing accidents during my police career where children were struck after crossing carelessly in front of a bus. It's something I always try to pass on if I'm delivering driver training.

The scenario is this: A bus stops at the nearside kerb on a busy road. A passenger gets off the bus, intending to cross the road, but instead of walking to the rear of the bus, they walk *in front* of the bus, which is still stopped & picking up passengers.

They then emerge, unexpectedly, from the front of the bus into traffic which is overtaking the stationary bus. If they're lucky, the passing drivers will see them and react. If they're not, they'll be hit. Both of the children I dealt with died as a result.

As a driver, these pedestrians are particularly difficult to spot. You may be moving to the offside to pass the bus, so you've no view of the nearside kerb, or the pedestrian as they get off the bus. You'll have no view of their feet under the bus because if the size of the vehicle, which is also why you won't see them through any of the buses windows.

In America, when a school bus stops to let children on or off, it is against the law to pass the bus in *both* directions. The bus stops, and all traffic, in both directions, *must* stop, to prevent this type of accident from happening.

In the UK, the best advice is to pass stationary buses as wide and slow as possible and to always be aware of the possibility that someone may try to cross from the front of the bus.

In Conclusion

If you think along these lines, and keep these considerations to the forefront of your mind when there are pedestrians around, you're far more likely to spot the *one* deaf, drunk, phone reading, umbrella wielding pedestrian *before* they get the chance to leap on your bonnet. And remember - it only takes one.

7. Vision affected by external factors (11% of all accidents)

Stationary or parked vehicle(s)   **3%**

3% of all accidents involve a stationary or parked vehicle. The majority of those accidents involve a pedestrian, because the biggest risk with stationary or parked vehicles is that they are very good at hiding pedestrians – particularly children.

If you're driving past a line of parked vehicles – irrespective of which side of the road they're parked on – there is always a possibility that a pedestrian will step out between two of the vehicles into your path. Larger vehicles are more effective at hiding pedestrians, but even very small cars can completely mask a child or a small adult right up until the point where they leap out in front of your moving car...

There are, however, some straightforward observation techniques you can use to help you spot pedestrians before they step out, and some actions you can take in relation to your speed and position which will keep the possibility of mowing down a careless pedestrian to a minimum.

Where should you look?

Firstly, don't confine your forward observations solely to the road ahead of you. Instead, move your eyes – and even your head – from side to side and use your peripheral vision to scan onto the footpaths on the other sides of the parked cars. Keep looking left and right as well as straight ahead and look into any driveways, entrances, side roads and car parks as you approach them. Look for any signs of movement & be ready to react to them if necessary.

In addition, you should continually scan underneath the parked vehicles – often an under-vehicle view will allow you to see feet, or the movement of feet when no other parts of a pedestrian are visible. If those feet are moving towards the road, again, be ready to take some sort of action if necessary.

Be particularly careful in the vicinity of schools at starting/finishing times and around or near parked food vans, ice-cream vans etc. As the old public information film used to say "children are more interested in ice-cream than they are in crossing the road safely" (or something like that!)

Be aware that pedestrians sometimes get off buses and cross in front of the bus, instead of behind it, so always pass stationary buses wide and slow and be prepared to stop.

You should also be cautious of cars which have just pulled over and stopped ahead of you, as the driver and passengers may get out of the car carelessly.

What should I do?

If you use the observation tips above and you spot what you think is a pedestrian about to step into the road, you've a few options – doing nothing is *not* an option though, so please be ready to take some kind of action.

Firstly, move away from them. If the pedestrian is on the nearside (left side) of the road, you should move as far to the offside (right) as you can safely go. This will give you and the pedestrian a little more room should they step out.

You should be prepared to stop, and you shouldn't be travelling at a speed which won't allow you to stop should someone step out. Keep your speed reasonable when passing cars and remember all the stuff about emergency braking from chapter 1 – if they do step out, make sure you press that brake pedal as quickly and as hard as you can physically manage. Use all the car's braking ability and don't forget to steer around them whilst you're braking as well.

If you spot the pedestrian early enough and you think they're about to step out, give them a horn warning. I've mentioned elsewhere that horns are drastically underused (and misused) in the UK, and warning a pedestrian – who you've assessed as probably being unaware of your approach – is an entirely correct use of the horn.

Be careful with your timing of the horn though – if you give them a blast *after* they have stepped out, they may react by stopping or trying to change direction, which could make things worse for you, so only give a horn warning if you spot someone *before* they step out.

Other stationary vehicle issues

There are other risks associated with stationary or parked vehicles – one of the biggest risks involves roads where you wouldn't normally expect to encounter stationary vehicles – motorways, dual carriageways and clearways.

Motorways are – mile for mile – statistically by far the safest roads in the country if you consider how many miles are travelled and how many vehicles use the motorway network. But accidents do happen on motorways and because of the speeds at which motorway traffic travels, when an accident *does* happen, it tends to be a serious and/or multiple vehicle accident.

The other interesting statistic (in terms of this book, anyway) relating to motorways is that the majority of *fatal* accidents occur on the hard shoulder.

In recent years, you may have noticed that whenever you see a vehicle broken down on the hard shoulder, you'll usually see a miserable, wet, shivering driver & passengers stood away from the vehicle, on the other side of the Armco barrier, often half-way up the grass embankment.

But why? Why don't they just wait in their car, out of the wind and rain?

It's because there is a real risk that another vehicle will simply drive into their car whilst it's stationary on the hard shoulder.

The recovery operators always insist that anyone in the vehicle gets out and waits in a safe place – well away from the motorway and the stationary car, so that they're not hurt or killed if someone drives into their car.

But how could anyone be bloody stupid or careless enough to drive into a broken down car which is stopped where it should be – on the hard shoulder?

It's because of a phenomenon called *target fixation*.

Target fixation is a reaction – often suffered by people who have been driving long distances at high speeds – whereby they see something, stare at it (to the exclusion of everything else around them) and involuntarily drive straight at the thing they're staring at.

It was first recognised by doctors studying the reactions of fighter pilots who would occasionally attack a target, but then fail to "pull out of the dive" and fly straight into their target.

There's an easy way to avoid target fixation – keep your wits about you on long, boring journeys and keep moving your eyes around, without fixing on one thing for too long. The one thing you *mustn't* do when driving on the motorway is stare intently at the car in front of you – this is the primary cause of target fixation – people are used to staring at the car in front and when they transfer their stare to a stationary vehicle on the hard shoulder, they fail to realise – for a shot but crucial period – that the vehicle *isn't* moving.

Usually, by the time they realise, it's too late to do anything about it.

If you suffer a breakdown or other emergency on the motorway, there is one thing you must try your absolute best to avoid:

If at all possible, you should **never stop in a live "running" lane on the motorway**. Do everything you possibly can to stop on the hard shoulder, as far to the left as is possible.

Most breakdowns occur whilst your car is still moving at some speed, so if the engine cuts out and the dashboard lights up like Christmas, don't just stop immediately – put the car in neutral or dip the clutch, switch on your hazard lights and do everything you can to move across to lane 1 and then onto the hard shoulder.

If you can, you should keep coasting until you get to an emergency telephone box – these are situated every mile along the motorway and although you may well have a mobile phone, an emergency telephone box will automatically inform the operator of your exact location and they'll be able to get recovery to you as quickly as possible.

Take the operators advice, get everyone out of the car and over the barrier as soon as possible & leave lights and hazards switched on.

If you're travelling on a "managed" or "smart" motorway which use the hard shoulder as a running lane, you should try to stop in one of the refuge areas (small layby-type areas) which are placed at regular intervals on the left.

If you cannot stop in a refuge and you have no choice other than to stop in a live lane, you should switch on your hazard warning lights and if possible, get out of your car via the left hand door and wait behind the barrier. If you can't get out of your car, if you don't think it's safe to get out, or if there is no other place of relative safety, stay in the vehicle. Keep your seat belt on and dial '999'.

The main thing to do is to stay calm, don't panic and call for help. Managed motorways are constantly monitored by CCTV cameras and as soon as you stop, the control room operator will take action to close the lane you're in and keep you as safe as possible.

Where do you park?

You should always give some careful thought to where you leave your car parked – particularly if it's by the side of the road.

I see so many cars parked up which make me wonder "what the ruddy hell were they thinking?". Cars parked on blind crests, on corners, across junctions and blocking emergency access routes. I sometimes find it hard to believe that people can really be that careless or inconsiderate.

But they are – not usually with any malicious intent – but because, like most of us, they're simply caught up in their own thoughts about their errand or their visit or their shopping.

Don't be that idiot!

Give a little thought to where you're going to park and whether it's going to cause any difficulty for other road users. Have you left enough room for vehicles to get past? Are you blocking anyone's access? Could a fire engine get past if it needed to (it will get past if it needs to, believe me, but your car might end up badly damaged if you haven't left enough room!).

When you have parked and you've got out of your car, have a look at it and go through the same considerations again. What would you think if you were driving past? Would you find it difficult to pass? Would its position cause you any problems?

A few second's thought can make a real difference – I only wish more people would go through this process when they park!

Dazzling sun   3%

This was quite a surprise to me – almost 3000 accidents caused every year, in part by drivers being dazzled by the sun.

I mean – we live in the UK – when did you last see the sun? I think it was a Tuesday sometime last August!

The sun can be a problem though – particularly when it is low on the horizon and you're driving towards it. It can be particularly bad at sunrise and sunset in winter when the roads are damp and very reflective. If you've been driving in one direction and you turn a corner or at a junction directly into a setting sun with a damp road surface, the brightness can sometimes almost blind you and it certainly affects your ability to see everything you need to when you're driving.

Until they invent a dimmer switch for the sun, I don't really have much advice to help you with this one, apart from the obvious, so here goes...

Use your flip-down sun visors when the sun is low in the sky to keep it from dazzling you and keep a pair of sunglasses in the car within easy reach at all times.

If you absolutely cannot avoid driving into a setting or rising sun, avoid looking directly at the sun, as this will cause temporary "flashes" of blindness in your eyes which could take up to a few minutes to fade. Instead, look away from the sun and keep moving your eyes around the whole environment.

If your vision is badly affected, slow down, but don't brake hard or suddenly, because the drivers behind will also be dazzled by the sun and may not see you braking until it's too late.

Driving into the sun also highlights how dirty your windscreen is – particularly in winter when the roads are salty – so you can expect a number of cars in front to start washing their windscreens.

Rain, sleet, snow, or fog   2%

You'd think this one would cause far more accidents than dazzling sunlight, wouldn't you? It's just a description of normal British weather! In this case, however, the contributory factor refers to *vision* affected by rain, sleet, snow or fog, so I suppose the fact that we see more of these types of weather than anything else means that we've trained ourselves to see more effectively in rain than in bright sunshine...

Rain

Depressingly, rain is the most common condition we're likely to come across in the UK, so let's look at how you can stay safe when it's raining. Firstly, you need to be able to see out of your car as effectively as possible, so it's important to keep your glass clean on the inside and outside & replace your wipers when they start to streak.

Keep a little airflow over your windscreen at all times – my preference is to leave the air conditioning turned on all year round, because it dries the air inside the car and prevents the windows from steaming up. So even when it's cold, keep the air conditioning on with your heater and the warm air will be nicely dried and will keep your windows from steaming up.

Don't be tempted to wipe mist from the inside of your windows with a leather, cloth or sleeve – it will streak badly and will affect your vision. Just wait a second or two and let your heater & A/C do the work.

The amount of rain hitting the windscreen increases with your speed. Use your windscreen wipers as a guide to whether your speed is appropriate. If it's raining *very* hard and you have your wipers on maximum speed, but you cannot properly see because of the amount of rain on your windscreen, you should slow down until your vision improves.

Use dipped headlights (but NOT fog lights) when it's raining to make yourself more visible to other road users.

On faster roads such as motorways, heavy spray from other vehicles can often be more of a hindrance to good visibility than the rain itself. Tyres are very efficient at clearing water these days which means they're much grippier in wet weather than they used to be, but that water has to go somewhere. It's generally thrown up behind the vehicle in a large plume of spray which can badly affect vision.

When it's raining, you should increase your following position from the vehicle in front. In dry conditions, a 2 second gap is usually fine, but in wet conditions a 2 second gap could put you right in the middle of that plume of spray and effectively leave you almost completely blind.

Instead, drop back to 4, or even 6 seconds behind the vehicle in front – as far back as you need to be to maintain good vision.

Many people sit on the motorway in heavy rain & heavy spray from other vehicles, thinking that visibility is absolutely awful. This is because the majority of drivers concentrate solely on what the vehicle in front is doing, and they fail to look at the bigger picture.

The next time you're travelling in very wet conditions, instead of trying to watch the vehicle in front, try looking much further ahead – look around the vehicles in front, along the gaps in between vehicles and between the motorway lanes. When you crest a hill, look over the top of all the vehicles in front and try to look as far along the motorway as possible.

I've sat alongside drivers who think that visibility is almost zero, when, in fact, if they were looking in the right places, they could see in excess of a mile ahead. And that extended view gives you plenty of warning about when the traffic ahead might need to slow, so that you don't end up slamming the brakes on unexpectedly.

Fog, sleet & snow

When it comes to your vision, fog, sleet & snow are tricky. Let's start with fog - it's effectively cloud which has dropped to ground level and it can be thick, thin, misty, patchy and usually a combination of any or all of these.

I've written some advice on the correct use of lights and fog lights elsewhere in the book, but it's worth repeating here. To start with – make sure you're at least displaying dipped headlights when it's foggy – that should be the absolute minimum and it's amazing how many people don't even bother with this basic requirement.

There is a school of thought which suggests that a combination of front fog lights and sidelights is most effective in thick fog. Even the legislation allows for this, giving an exemption from dipped headlights on non-30mph limit roads if it's foggy & you're displaying a sidelight/fog light combination.

The problem with driving in fog is that any bright light you display to the front is reflected back at you by the fog itself (or by the tiny water droplets which make up fog if you want to be technical).

I've tried the sidelight/fog light combination in a number of cars and I've never really found it much better than just headlights, and I've often found it worse. The idea is that the low front fog lights project a beam across the road surface, whilst the sidelights prevent excessive light reflection from the fog. Sounds good in theory, but it's not great in reality.

A note on intelligent use of fog lights - many people see mist or fog and then just switch their fog lights on as a sort of automatic response & leave them on for the rest of the journey. In reality, the occasions you actually need to use fog lights are extremely limited. Visibility of less than 100 metres is extremely thick fog or very

heavy snowfall (the only two weather conditions which would require high intensity fog light use) and those weather conditions are quite rare.

You don't need fog lights when it's a bit misty, or there's a bit of dampness in the air, and you definitely *never* need them when it's raining, no matter how torrentially, because the extra glare caused by fog lights reflecting off a wet road create more dangers rather than less.

If you are driving in less than 100M visibility, your rear fog lights are important to ensure traffic approaching from the rear can see you, but once you can see the headlights of following traffic in your mirror, it's usually best to switch off your fog lights, because if you can see their headlights, they'll be able to see your tail lights without fog light assistance. Don't forget that rear fog lights can mask your brake lights and make it more likely that a following vehicle will not see when you are slowing down.

Fog can be patchy too, so switch the fogs on just when they are needed and switch them off as soon as it's clear again.

And remember - they are *fog* lights – **NOT** driving lamps, posing lamps or fashion accessories. If you're not in thick fog or snow, leave them switched off!

Don't forget that fog is actually just tiny droplets of water and will settle on your windscreen. Use the wipers – front and rear – regularly to keep your screen as clear as possible.

And don't fall into the trap of just following the car in front. Your vision might be badly reduced by the fog, but try to keep scanning past the car in front, and as far into the distance as you can.

Freezing fog

Freezing fog isn't much different from normal fog really, but freezing fog occurs when it is very cold and the tiny droplets which make up the fog are mad of ice, rather than water.

In freezing fog, the icy droplets can settle on the road surface and make it slippery, so be aware of your grip levels.

You also need to set your heater on a high heat setting, blowing on your windscreen and keep your rear demister on. The freezing fog can settle on your glass and ice up very quickly, so it's important to keep your glass warm and free from ice.

Sleet & Snow

You should only use fog lights in sleet & snow if visibility is reduced to less than 100 metres. If it is, follow my advice above in relation to sensible and intelligent use of the fog lights and monitor how heavy the snow or sleet is & switch off your fog lights when visibility starts to improve.

Vehicle blind spot   1%

Every vehicle has a number of blind spots. Blind spots are the areas around the vehicle which, although they're quite close to the vehicle, are out of view to the driver in their normal driving position (i.e. when the driver is just sat at the wheel, using his/her mirrors).

In a car there are blind spots immediately in front and behind (right in front of the front bumper and immediately behind the rear bumper), behind the vehicles pillars (front, side and rear) and in an area to the side and rear of the vehicle which isn't generally covered by the rear-view mirrors.

It's important to be aware of the positions, so that you know where, when and how to check them, and so that you are aware of *other vehicles'* blind spots when you're on the move.

Vehicle blind spots (or, more accurately, the driver's failure to check them properly) are at least partly responsible for a number of highly publicised fatal accidents involving cyclists in London and other cities over the last few years. There is a fantastic short video on Youtube (search for "TFL lorry blind spot") which demonstrates why blind spots can be so dangerous.

It is filmed firstly from the point of view of the driver of an articulated lorry – the driver looks in their nearside (left) mirrors and can only see the nearside kerb and the side of his lorry. The driver then gets out of his cab, walks round the front of the vehicle and, in actual fact, there are over 10 cyclists, all wearing high-vis, lined up two-abreast right next to the lorry – clearly in a very vulnerable position should the lorry turn left.

I know that this book is primarily aimed at car drivers, but your nearside and offside "over shoulder" blind spots are bigger than you might think and, in many cases, are big enough to hide entire cars, so it's important that you're aware of the blind spots and that you know how to check them properly.

Firstly, you should make sure your mirrors are adjusted properly. When you're sat in your car, without shifting in your seat, have a look in your side (door) mirrors. What can you see? You can significantly reduce the size of your vehicle's blind spots by adjusting your mirrors correctly, so if you can see mostly the side of your car and the road surface, they're way out!

Sitting with your head in the normal position for driving, adjust your door mirrors so that the part of the mirror nearest to the car (the left side of your right mirror and vice-versa for the left mirror) shows no more than about 10% of the side of your car. So the mirror should just show a small portion of the side of your car down the edge closest to the car, and the rest should show the road to the rear.

In the remaining 90% of the mirror view, you should be able to see the road to the rear. I don't mean *just* the road surface – you should have a good view into the distance behind – the horizon should be roughly across the centre of the mirror.

If you set your mirrors in this way, you'll reduce the size of your blind spots to a minimum.

Shoulder Checks

Ask motorcyclists about shoulder checks and they'll tell you that they are a life saver. Shoulder checks are actually referred to as "life savers" in many motorcycle training manuals and courses, such is the importance placed on them.

They are, in fact, just as important for car drivers as they are for motorcyclists. The only way to effectively and efficiently check that there is definitely nothing hiding in your blind spots is to physically look over both shoulders. And I don't mean a quick turn of your head – I mean physically turning in your seat and looking *right* over your left and right shoulders – right into the areas not covered by your car's mirrors.

I always teach learner drivers to perform left and right shoulder checks every time they set off from stationary, to check for the cyclist or motorcyclist who might be filtering slowly past, or for the vehicle which might have pulled up alongside without them noticing.

As you build your driving experience, you might find that your rear observations improve and that you don't necessarily feel as though a shoulder check is necessary every time you set off from stationary, but I think it's good advice and if you absolutely want to make sure there's nothing there, you should check over your shoulders.

When you're driving along the motorway – particularly when you've just joined the motorway – there is a real possibility that vehicles could be hidden in your blind spots. Before you leave the slip road to join lane 1, and before you change lanes to the right, you should always carry out a right shoulder check – it is surprising how some very large vehicles can be completely hidden in your blind spots & changing lanes in front of an overtaking vehicle rarely ends well.

In addition, it's always good practice to carry out a quick right-shoulder check just as you're about to leave the motorway & join an exit slip road. Some drivers and riders can make last-minute, badly planned exits from the motorway at speed – often within the confines of your blind spots, so a right shoulder check just before you join the exit slip road is very good practice.

Vehicle Pillars

The pillars are the parts of a cars body which hold the roof up – cars generally have pillars at each corner and most have pillars in the middle as well – in between the front and rear doors or to the rear of the front doors.

As car manufacturers have been required to make cars safer and safer, pillars have got thicker and thicker. There are good reasons for this – old cars had thin pillars and if they rolled over in an accident, it was very likely that the roof would collapse and the occupants would be seriously injured.

These days, in a modern car with thick pillars, the occupants are much safer in the event of a roll-over accident, but the downside is that the thicker pillars – particularly the front, or "A" pillars, create significant blind-spots which can hide cyclists and motorcyclists from view.

If you're waiting at a junction and your view is partially obstructed by a pillar, you should move around in your seat – lean forwards and back – to make sure you have seen fully behind your pillars and you haven't missed an approaching vehicle.

Be aware of other driver's blind spots

Have you ever seen a sticker on the back of a lorry or bus which says something like "if you cannot see my mirrors, I cannot see you"?

That's a hint that you should be aware of *your own* visibility to other road users. So far, we've discussed how to check your own blind spots for hidden vehicles, but how do you know that *other* drivers will correctly check their blind spots for *your* vehicle?

The truth is that you don't know, and in many cases, they won't, so you should look to improve your awareness of the position of other driver's blind spots and avoid sitting in them for any length of time.

So, for example, if you're sitting in lane 2 of the motorway in fairly heavy traffic, you're not making much progress and your speed is matched to the vehicles in lane 1, you should think carefully about where you position yourself in relation to the vehicles in lane 1.

The *worst* place to sit is on the vehicle's rear three-quarters – with the front of your vehicle alongside the rear passenger doors or boot of the vehicle in lane 1. If you sit there, you're right in their blind spot and there is a real danger that they cannot see you and they may change lanes right into the side of you.

Instead, you should sit in a position where you're either slightly ahead of their line of sight – at least in front of their side window, or in a position further behind, where if they moved lanes, they wouldn't come into contact with you.

When you're passing heavy goods vehicles or buses, be aware that their blind spots are much larger and can sometimes hide several cars. Don't sit "alongside" moving vehicles – instead sit slightly ahead or behind them. If you're passing them, use a squirt of acceleration to get fully past them as quickly as possible & keep your "time alongside" to a minimum.

If you train yourself to have an awareness of other vehicles' blind spots, you'll keep yourself out of those dangerous areas as much as possible and keep the chances of being involved in someone else's accident to a minimum.

Road layout (e.g. bend, winding road, hill crest) 1%

Vegetation   **0%**
(345)

Buildings, road signs, street furniture   **0%**
(233)

Yes, road layouts, vegetation and street furniture can affect your vision, but there is one overriding safety "rule" which, if you apply in all circumstances, will ensure that you're never caught out by a road layout which affects your vision:

You should always be able to stop, on your own side of the road, in the distance you can see to be clear.

It's an old and well-used advanced driving mantra, but it's one of the best rules to keep in the back of your mind. If you constantly think to yourself – as part of your observation and planning process – "could I stop", you'll ensure that you're never travelling too fast to stop when the unexpected happens.

It doesn't mean you have to crawl around everywhere at 3mph. Modern cars and modern tyres provide extremely effective braking and if you ever get the chance to try your brakes to their full capacity in a safe environment, you'll be amazed at how quickly your car will stop when you use the brakes to their full effect.

So, your driving plan should always include the question "could I stop?" It doesn't have to be pretty, or smooth, or progressive – you just need to be able to stop in an emergency with a full application of the brakes.

So, if you're approaching a bend with limited vision, you should slow down to a speed where you know you could stop *only in the distance you can see to be clear.*

Keep this rule in mind every time you go out for a drive.

Dazzling headlights   0%

Main beam headlights are extremely effective at illuminating the road ahead, and good drivers will use them considerately, dipping their lights whenever an oncoming vehicle comes into view so as not to dazzle the other driver.

Many drivers, however, fail to give this simple courtesy and will merrily drive towards you at night with their lights on full beam, either oblivious to the fact that they're blinding you, or just not caring.

If you are dazzled by an oncoming vehicle, what's the best course of action? It's very tempting to give them a taste of their own medicine and burn out their retinas too, but do you really want two partially-blinded drivers driving towards each other at speed?

The best advice is to look slightly away from the headlights. Shining a bright light into your eyes creates a "flash blindness" which is a sort of blob of blindness in one part of your eye, similar to when a camera flash goes off. This flash spot can remain for a few seconds or minutes, so it's best to look away slightly from the lights so that your flash blindness occurs in an area outside your main field of vision. Try to look to the left of the oncoming car - towards the nearside kerb.

If you want to indicate to the oncoming vehicle that they are a main beam numpty, try my courtesy signal of switching to sidelights a couple of times. This will flash your lights without causing excessive dazzle and might wake them up.

If the car behind is the problem, almost all cars are fitted with dipping rear-view mirrors which dim the appearance of following traffic. If you're a company director type, you may even have an automatic dipping mirror, but for most of us mere mortals, the mirror can be dipped by flicking the lever underneath the mirror, or in the case of BMWs, turning the red alarm light under the mirror.

Spray from other vehicles   0%

On faster roads such as motorways & dual carriageways, heavy spray from other vehicles can often be more of a hindrance to good visibility than the rain itself. Tyres are very efficient at clearing water these days which means they're much grippier in wet weather than they used to be, but that water has to go somewhere. It's generally thrown up behind the vehicle in a large plume of spray which can badly affect vision.

When it's raining, you should increase your following position from the vehicle in front. In dry conditions, a 2 second gap is usually fine, but in wet conditions a 2 second gap could put you right in the middle of that plume of spray and effectively leave you almost completely blind.

Instead, drop back to 4, or even 6 seconds behind the vehicle in front – as far back as you need to be to maintain good vision.

Many people sit on the motorway in heavy rain & heavy spray from other vehicles, thinking that visibility is absolutely awful. This is because the majority of drivers concentrate solely on whet the vehicle in front is doing, and they fail to look at the bigger picture.

The next time you're travelling in very wet conditions, instead of trying to watch the vehicle in front, try looking much further ahead – look around the vehicles in front, along the gaps in between vehicles and between the motorway lanes. When you crest a hill, look over the top of all the vehicles in front and try to look as far along the motorway as possible.

I've sat alongside drivers who think that visibility is almost zero, when, in fact, if they were looking in the right places, they could see in excess of a mile ahead. And that extended view gives you plenty of warning about when the traffic ahead might need to slow, so that you don't end up slamming the brakes on unexpectedly.

Visor or windscreen dirty, scratched or frosted etc. 0%

This is one of those contributory factors which could end with my advice sounding very patronising, but here goes!

Keeping your windscreen clear is, of course vitally important. Firstly, keep your windscreen wipers in good condition and replace them as soon as they start to smear, or leave small streaks on your windscreen.

Keep your windscreen washer bottle topped up and use water mixed with an additive to make sure the bottle doesn't freeze solid on cold nights.

I like to use a water-repellent coating on all my car's windows, which encourages rain and spray to "bead" and run off the car, rather than settle until it is wiped off.

On frosty mornings, you'll often see people driving along, having scraped a 2" square clear patch, through which they can see with one eye. If they squint. You don't need me to tell you that this is daft and, of course, very dangerous.

On a very cold morning, instead of scraping the ice off your car for 10 minutes, or using one of those chemical sprays, I just use warm water. Get a jug of warm (not boiling – this could cause cracks) water and pour it over your windscreen and other windows. If you use a water repellent coating, the water will melt the ice and then run off completely, leaving a lovely clear windscreen.

Be aware that any remaining water can re-freeze on the windscreen if it's really cold, so avoid using your wipers until the car has completely warmed up.

8. SPECIAL CODES (5% OF ALL ACCIDENTS)

Other   3%

"Other" is included in the list of contributory factors to account for the fact that, no matter how many factors you put on the list, someone will invariably have an accident which no-one ever thought could, or might happen. It allows the reporting officer to select "other" when nothing else seems to fit.

A colleague of mine once attended an injury accident where a driver had lost control because his girlfriend was performing what the tabloid newspapers refer to as "a sexual act" on him as he drove along. The injury was recorded as "a serious bite injury". I'll let you use your imagination to work out where he was bitten and how upset he was!

Emergency vehicle on a call   0% (578)

I've explained elsewhere that drivers of emergency vehicles can, and do sometimes get things wrong at traffic light junctions and that you should always be aware that these vehicles could pass through junctions *against* red traffic lights.

Emergency response drivers are well trained, but there is a tendency amongst other road users to panic when they see approaching blue flashing lights and sirens. Believe me – as someone who has driven many thousands of miles under emergency blue lights – this is the last thing they want you to do.

Yes, they may be on their way to an emergency incident, and yes, that incident may be a life-or death situation, but the emergency driver's priority is *to get there.* If they have an accident on route, another vehicle will have to be dispatched, and *another* vehicle will have to be dispatched to the accident, so crashing on route to an emergency is genuinely something to be avoided at all costs!

Emergency response drivers are taught to remain calm, to deal with traffic and other situations as they find it, and they're also taught the most common reactions of other drivers. So let's look at some of those common reactions, and how you can avoid them.

The first thing to bear in mind is that the emergency drivers want you to help them to get past, but they don't expect you to do anything silly, or dangerous, to allow them to do so. I used to see people diving up kerbs (which must have damaged their wheels), onto grass verges (at the risk of becoming stuck) and actually crashing into other cars in order to get out of my way on an emergency blue-light run.

I really – honestly – never wanted them to do any of these things. If it came down to the fact that there was simply nowhere for people to go to get out of my way, I'd even switch off my blue lights and sirens occasionally so that traffic could calm down & get moving again. When it did, and when there was somewhere for people to move to, I'd switch on the blues 'n twos again and pass where it was safe.

If you see an emergency vehicle approaching from your rear, look well ahead for a place to move over so that they can get past you safely. You might not need to stop – the road might be wide enough for you to move left and slow down – but give a signal if you do, so that the emergency driver knows you're actually moving for them (and you're not about to do an unexpected "U" turn in the road – something which happened to me on more than one occasion).

Many drivers just move over and stop when they see the blue lights behind, but without thinking about the fact that the priority for the emergency driver is *to get past.* So some will stop next to a central reservation, or alongside parked cars, or halfway round a roundabout. They stop in places where it's impossible for the emergency vehicle to get past and although their intentions are good, they actually end up hindering the progress of the emergency vehicle, rather than helping it.

So don't just pull over at the first opportunity – make sure you're pulling over somewhere where the emergency vehicle will be able to pass you safely.

On motorways and dual carriageways, sirens of vehicles approaching from the rear are much more difficult -and often impossible – to hear, so it's important that you keep up with good, regular mirror checks. When traffic is flowing, the emergency driver's preference is to pass you in the offside lane, so please pull into a lane to your left and don't slow in the right-most lane, expecting the emergency vehicle to pass you on the left.

The best piece of advice when you see an emergency vehicle with blue lights displayed is to stay calm, think about what the emergency driver wants to do, and make a sensible, considered decision about how best to help them in getting past. Don't do anything sudden or unpredictable & try to give the driver a signal that you've seen them and are reacting to them.

If you're passed by an emergency vehicle responding to an incident, always be aware that there might be another one behind it. Travelling in convoy is always quite risky for emergency drivers, because other drivers will see and react to the first vehicle, and then set off again when it's passed, without appreciating that there is a second vehicle immediately behind it.

Vehicle door opened or closed negligently   1%

This is a fairly easy one to cover in a couple of paragraphs! Make sure you look behind you properly before opening your door in traffic, by checking your mirrors and giving a shoulder check before opening your door. Be particularly mindful of cyclists as they tend to pass parked cars quite closely.

If you've got passengers in the car, make sure you know what they're doing and tell them to wait before getting out of the car. If you've got children in the rear, it's always a good idea to make sure the car's child-locks are switched on, so that the doors cannot be opened from the inside.

Be particularly careful on windy days. A strong gust of wind can easily catch a door as it's being opened and swing it out of your grasp very quickly. Take a good, firm grip of the door handle as you open the door and make sure you're holding it tight as you start to open it.

When you're passing a row of parked cars, it's always best – if there's enough room – to leave at least a door's width between your car and the parked cars. Imagine the parked cars' doors fully open & try to leave at least that much room between your car and them – that way, if a door does unexpectedly open into your path, it won't hit your car.

If this isn't possible, you should pass parked cars reasonably slowly, and look out for clues that a door may open. Look for head movements in cars, brake lights going off, and doors which look like they're *not quite* shut properly.

Stolen vehicle   1% (598)
Vehicle in course of crime   0% (440)

I've bundled these two contributory factors together because the issues are the same – these factors relate mostly to vehicles which crash, or cause crashes whilst escaping the scene of a crime or whilst trying to evade the police.

The one thing I'm not going to do is describe police tactics in detail to help out car thieves and getaway drivers! So if you've bought this book to find out how to evade the cops I'm afraid you're looking in the wrong place!

One observation I will share with you, which is based on many years dealing with the criminal classes in general, and with drivers who have tried to evade arrest, is that these people are *by far* the most dangerous drivers on the road.

They have one aim, and one aim alone – to escape the police – and they will do absolutely anything, no matter how dangerous or reckless, to achieve this aim.

I've seen drivers go on to the opposite carriageways of motorways, drive on the wrong sides of roundabouts and the wrong way down one-way streets to avoid arrest. I've had bricks, bottles, shoes, and even a fridge thrown at my police car from fleeing vehicles and I've seen pursued drivers deliberately ram other vehicles in order to escape arrest.

In other words, unless you're a specially trained (advanced and pursuit trained) police officer in a suitable car, you should do everything you possibly can to avoid these types of drivers.

Now, fortunately, these types of incident are actually pretty rare – despite what you might think after watching another episode of "road wars" – but it's useful to know what to do if you think you're about to be passed by a car which is being pursued by the police.

If you spot the warning signs early enough – blue lights, sirens, more than one emergency vehicle close together and a vehicle ahead of them driving at high speed and possibly erratically – there is just one thing you should do...

Get as far out of the way as soon as you possibly can.

Unlike emergency vehicles on a response run, fleeing criminals do not have safety in mind and will not be taking the precautions usually taken by emergency service drivers. If necessary, they'll even ram you out of the way to make progress, so the best advice if you see a pursuit approaching – either from behind or in front – is to pull over as far as you can and get out of the way.

Pull on to the pavement if it's safe to do so, or turn off into the next junction. I'd even pull into someone's driveway if I could to avoid a pursuit – anything you can sensibly do, as quickly as possible to get out of the way.

I occasionally encountered a "have a go hero" who would try to use their car to deliberately block the fleeing vehicle. Although their intentions were always honourable, this is extremely dangerous and should be avoided at all costs. You never know how the fleeing driver will react, and you may get in the way of a planned tactical manoeuvre which is being planned by the police, so please, do not get involved!

9. VEHICLE DEFECTS (2% OF ALL ACCIDENTS)

Accidents caused by vehicle defects are quite rare – only 2% of all accidents are caused by defective vehicles, but it's worth looking at each of these contributory factors, how to avoid the defects, how to spot them before they cause an accident and how to deal with them if they occur whilst you're driving.

Defective brakes   1%

Brake failure can be a very frightening experience – we use the brakes when we want to slow down or stop, so imagine for a second that you press the pedal and nothing happens – what would you do? How would you react? How would you bring the car to a stop?

Let's start with something far less exciting – maintenance. It's really important that you have your car – and your brakes –

serviced and maintained regularly. Brakes are designed to gradually wear out, so the friction surfaces – the discs and pads – or the shoes and drums – will wear out with use and need replacing.

How often? That's impossible to answer and depends on how hard you use your brakes, how heavy your car is and how fast you drive. Brake pads can last as little as 5,000 miles with heavy use and as long as 30,000 miles or more with gentle use. Discs generally last a bit longer, but will also need replacing at some points during a car's life.

Some cars have "wear indicators" built in to the braking system – a light or warning message will appear in the cars dashboard to let you know that the brakes are ready for replacing. The warning will appear before your brakes are fully worn out, to allow you time to have them replaced, but – please – don't wait too long. If the wear indicator flashes on our dashboard, you should look to get your brakes serviced within the next 200 miles at most.

If your car doesn't have wear indicators, regular servicing within the manufacturers recommended intervals should spot any excessive wear to your brakes before they become defective – if your garage recommends replacing your brake pads or discs, take their advice. I know no-one likes spending money on maintaining their car, but it's much better than finding that your brakes suddenly don't work!

It's also important that you have your brake fluid changed regularly – usually every 2-3 years. Brake fluid is hygroscopic, which means that it slowly absorbs small amounts of moisture from the air over long periods of time. If left unchanged for a long time, this moisture can cause something called "vapour lock", where the water becomes steam at high temperatures, which can cause a sudden, unexpected brake failure with the brake pedal going right to the floor.

Changing the brake fluid within the manufacturers recommended intervals will avoid vapour lock.

Even if you maintain your brakes to a high standard, there is always a small chance that one of the components in the braking system could fail and leave you without brakes. Introducing a momentary brake test into your driving can help you to spot a major brake failure before you set off.

It's not complicated – there are two simple brake tests you can carry out, starting with a stationary brake test.

This is easy – whenever you get in your car, before you do anything else – start the engine, put your seatbelt on, switch in the radio - just push the brake pedal. The pedal should be firm, with plenty of resistance after a small amount of movement. If the pedal goes soft or slowly (or quickly) sinks to the floor, there is very likely a serious fault with your brakes. Don't drive! Get someone to check your brakes and fix the fault before you drive the car again.

The second check is a moving brake test. When you first set off in your car, if there is no following traffic, give the brakes a gentle squeeze once you're up to about 20mph. The brakes should pull firmly in a straight line without pulling to the left or right.

If there is following traffic, just brake early for the first junction or hazard and make a note of how the brakes are working. If you're in any doubt, pull over and don't drive any further until you've had them checked over.

And if the brakes *do* fail?

Ok, so you've maintained your brakes properly and you've carried out a brake test and everything is fine, but during your journey, you press the brakes and nothing happens. You press them harder and the pedal goes to the floor – the car isn't slowing at all and you're approaching a line of stationary traffic. What do you do?

Firstly, don't panic! If you panic or freeze, you'll just plough into the stationary traffic with your foot planted on the non-operational brakes and your face frozen in a horrible expression.

Instead, keep your wits about you and try to work the problem – you need to stop the car.

Firstly, release the brake pedal and pump it a few times – sometimes pumping the brake pedal can restore enough braking efficiency to bring your car to a stop.

If this doesn't work, try the handbrake. The handbrake is usually mechanically connected to the rear wheels on a separate system from the service (foot) brake, so if your brakes have failed, your handbrake will usually still work.

Don't yank the handbrake with all your might though – it's usually connected to the rear wheels only and yanking it hard will lock the rear wheels solid. This won't slow you down much and could make your car spin out of control.

Instead, pull the lever up gently with the button depressed and steadily increase the pressure on the handbrake till the car starts to slow down. Even at high speeds, the handbrake can slow you quite efficiently if you use it correctly.

You can also use the cars gears to help you slow down – change down a couple of gears if you're in a manual car and the engine braking will help you to slow down.

If you've tried all these and you still think that you're going to crash into the stationary cars, you should look for the softest landing. Look for a barrier or wall to scrape along, or a hedge to drive into – anything apart from the other vehicles.

Apart from a tree. You should never drive into a tree. Even small trees don't move much when you drive into them!

Tyres illegal, defective or under inflated 1%

Most people completely fail to appreciate how important their tyres are. When you're driving, your tyres are the only parts of your car which are in contact with the road surface. Tyres are responsible for every movement that your car makes and every input you make with the cars controls is directly transferred to the car and the road surface through the tyres. They make your car accelerate, steer and brake as well as being responsible for supporting the full weight of the car, it's load and occupants whilst absorbing the worst of the bumps and potholes you'll find on every road these days.

Tyres need to be sufficiently "grippy" in all weather conditions to keep the car pointing where the driver wants to go. They also need to be *just* the right compound of rubber – too soft and they will wear out quickly. Too hard and they won't grip sufficiently well.

All-in-all, instead of being boring black circles of insignificant rubber, tyres are, in fact, by far the most important component of your car. So it's really important that you maintain them well to get the best out of them.

Let's start with tyre pressures, Tyres contain pressurised air and, over time, their pressures can drop. It's important that you check your tyre pressures every month or so to make sure they're consistent.

The correct tyre pressures for your car will be identified on a small sticker – it'll either be behind your fuel filler cap, or on one of the door jams (the area on the car which the door closes into). If you can't find it, the correct pressures will be printed in the owner's manual, or you'll be able to find them online.

Always stick to the manufacturers recommended pressures. If you drive with over, or under-inflated tyres, your braking, accelerating and steering capabilities will be greatly reduced and you'll increase the risk that you'll lose control of your car.

If you notice that one tyre is losing air pressure more quickly than the others, you may have a slow puncture or a leaking valve – best advice is to get it repaired or replaced as soon as possible, because a single tyre with low pressure can be even more dangerous than all four tyres with low pressure.

Whilst you're checking your tyre pressures, it's always worthwhile checking the condition of your tyres at the same time. Check that there are no cuts or bulges on the tread and on the sidewalls – particularly the inside sidewalls which aren't usually visible. Cuts or bulges can lead to sudden unexpected deflations or blowouts, which can be particularly dangerous.

Also check the wear on the tyre tread – tyres should wear evenly across the whole tread, so if you notice that one edge of the tyre is wearing more than the rest of the tyre, it could mean that your suspension is out of line and the tracking needs to be checked and corrected.

If the tyre is wearing on *both* edges, it could be an indication that your tyre pressures are too low, and if it is wearing excessively in the middle of the tread, it could mean that your tyre pressures are too high.

The legal requirement for tyre tread for cars in the UK is that they must have a minimum of 1.6mm of tread across the central ¾ of the width of the tyre, around the entire circumference. The outer 1/8 of the tyre tread can be less than 1.6mm, but must have visible tread remaining.

You can buy cheap tyre tread depth gauges which accurately measure the depth of the tread and are worth keeping in your glovebox, but tread depth can be checked for free without a gauge.

Manufacturers build "wear indicators" into the tyre tread – these are little bars of rubber which sit at the bottom of the tyre grooves at 3 or 4 points around the tyre. Once the rest of the tyre tread has worn down to these wear indicators, the tyre is no longer legal and needs replacing.

One word of warning though – the minimum tread depth of 1.6mm is very low and my advice is to change your tyres once they've worn down to a depth of 3mm. Any less than this and your tyres will not deal effectively with wet road surfaces and you could be putting yourself and your passengers at risk.

What if a tyre blows?

This is a common fear amongst people who regularly drive at speed on motorways and trunk roads – what if a tyre blows out suddenly and unexpectedly. Well, there's a couple of things to bear in mind before I go any further. Firstly, these types of incident are extremely rare – I've been driving for 30 years and I've driven many hundreds of thousands of miles sometimes at very high speeds, and I've never – once – experienced a sudden and unexpected tyre deflation.

The other thing to bear in mind is that if you check your tyres regularly as described above, you'll reduce your risks of a blow-out even further.

But, if the worst does come to the worst and one of your tyres lest go at speed, what can you expect? And what should you do?

The first thing you should know is that blow-outs happen very suddenly and very quickly. You may hear a bang, but the first thing you'll notice is that the car will suddenly – and quite forcefully want to veer off in the direction of the deflated tyre. Here's the bit where you need to keep your cool and work the problem properly.

Firstly - and probably most importantly – **DON'T BRAKE!** Braking will make things instantly 10 times worse and will probably result in the car rotating, completely out of your control.

Instead, take a firm grip of the steering wheel with both hands and keep the car pointing forwards. Lift off the accelerator and let the car start to slow down of its own accord. Steer gently towards the nearside – if you're on the motorway, stick in your left indicator and start moving across towards the hard shoulder. Other drivers will probably see that you're in difficulty and will, hopefully, give you room.

Once you're over to the left, or on the hard shoulder, put the car into neutral and let it coast to a halt. If you absolutely *have* to brake, you should do so as gently and smoothly as possible. Remember that braking will make the car steer strongly towards the punctured wheel, so increase your grip on the steering wheel and be prepared to counter-steer.

And once you've safely pulled over to the side of the road, take a moment to get your breath back and clean your trousers!

Defective steering or suspension   0% (315)

The advice I've already given about keeping your car well maintained is just as relevant to steering and suspension. If you have your car serviced regularly, within the manufacturers' recommended intervals, any steering or suspension faults should be picked up and fixed before they become a problem.

But if you do experience a steering failure whilst you're driving, I'm afraid there is very little you can do other than stop the car as soon as possible. Losing steering takes away most of your options when it comes to avoiding an accident, so - unlike the vast majority of scenarios I've described in this book – you'll be unable to direct the car away from a hazard if your steering breaks.

Best advice then, is just to stop as soon as possible using the brakes and try to use whatever steering control you've still got to get the car into a safe position.

One issue to remember with steering is that the vast majority of cars are fitted with power-assisted steering these days. With these systems, the steering is assisted by the engine via hydraulic pumps or electric motors, and the steering is kept relatively light and easy-to-operate.

When the engine cuts out, however, the power assistance is removed from the steering and it can feel as though the steering has failed completely and locked solid.

If your engine cuts out whilst you're travelling at speed, the steering will still work – it'll just need a lot more effort from the driver. So don't freeze and think you've lost all steering – grip the wheel hard with both hands and take control of the car whilst you bring it to a stop.

Suspension faults tend to result in a collapsing of the suspension at one corner of the car, or with a wheel suddenly pointing off in an odd direction. If this happens whilst you're moving, the wrong inputs can result in a bad situation becoming much worse.

If your car suddenly drops at one corner or lurches off to one side – remember my primary advice in the event of a blow out –

DON'T BRAKE! Instead, take a firm grip of the steering wheel with both hands and try to keep the car pointing in the right direction. You may hear all sorts of horrible grinding and crunching noises, but you just need to keep the car travelling straight and then try to bring it to a controlled stop by the side of the road. When you do use the brakes, use them smoothly, gently and progressively – any sudden or sharp braking could result in the car rotating out of control.

Overloaded or poorly loaded vehicle or trailer 0% (221)

There are very specific rules and regulations relating to how goods vehicles should be loaded and how much weight they can carry, but this isn't a book for lorry drivers, so I'll not be going into too much detail on the subject.

If you need to carry heavy or bulky items, you should make sure that your vehicle is suitable and that the load is secured in a way that it won't be a danger to you or anyone else on the roads.

If you tow a trailer, you should make sure that it is loaded evenly, with the weight distributed in such a way that it isn't excessively lifting, or weighing down the towing vehicle.

Defective lights or indicators   0% (183)
Defective or missing mirrors   0% (11)

I think we can cover these two in one straightforward, succinct section, don't you?!

Check your lights every month or so and replace any bulbs that have blown. Keep your mirrors clean and unobstructed and replace any mirrors or mirror glass which is broken.

Do I need to add anything further?

No – I don't think so either!

10. Are Driving Standards in the UK Getting Worse?

Are driving standards in the UK getting worse?

Yes.

And no.

The answer to this question is both subjective and objective. Without being more specific on what aspects of driving the question refers to, it's a very difficult question to answer, but let's look at the objective answer first.

The UK driving test is harder than it used to be, so if we look at this question purely in terms of the standards required to obtain a full UK car or motorcycle licence, then, without a doubt, driving standards in the UK have improved.

I know many of you won't believe that the driving test is harder, but these days a new driver has to pass a two-part test, the first of which requires an amount of study of the highway code and an amount of practice at hazard perception. The practical test is longer than it used to be, includes an element of "independent" driving and takes place on roads which are much busier than they used to be (more of this later). So yes, without question, the driving test is harder to pass than it used to be, which has resulted in newly-qualified drivers who are, on average, at a better standard than their counterparts 20, 30 or 40 years ago.

Whilst we're still on the objective answer, road casualties are also difficult to argue with. 7,000 road fatalities per year in the (pre driving test) 1930s when there were around 1,000,000 vehicles on the road, compared with around 1,500 per year in the 2010s with around 35,000,000 vehicles on the road. On their own, those figures should demonstrate a huge improvement in driving standards over the years.

The casualty figures have, however, been significantly improved by massive improvements in vehicle design, changes to legislation such as seatbelt and drink-driving laws, improved road design, street lighting etc. but somewhere in the mix, an improvement in driving standards has played a part in reducing the number of deaths on the road.

But then we get to the subjective answer. How do we *feel* about driving standards in the UK? Those of us who have been driving 25+ years generally feel like driving standards are getting worse year-on-year.

Having given it some considerable thought, I actually don't think that driving standards as a whole are any worse now than they were when I started driving in 1986. But - and this is a big but, so I'll capitalise it, embolden it etc. - **BUT** there are a lot more bad drivers on the road than there used to be.

How can this be? How can driving standards have improved, but there has also been an increase in bad drivers?

It's purely down to numbers. There has always been a proportion of drivers who are aggressive, inattentive, careless, ignorant, stupid or downright bloody-minded. As the number of vehicles on the road increases, the number of "those" drivers correspondingly increases. The behaviour of "those" drivers also seems to escalate based on how heavy or light the traffic is.

This leads to the misconception that driving standards are different in different parts of the country. Drive up to Northern Scotland, for instance, and you'll feel as though you're in the land of the excellent driver - you'll encounter very low levels of muppetry and you'll thoroughly enjoy the experience. You might come across the odd one or two clowns, but one or two won't ruin your day will they?

Drive inside the M60 at peak times and you'll feel like you've found another level of purgatory. Every few minutes you'll be cut up, hacked up, brake tested, swerved at and generally subjected to a mental battering by loads of idiots who seem like they're off their medication.

Are there more bad drivers on the roads of Greater Manchester than Northern Scotland? Yes, of course. But that's not the right question to ask.

The right question should be "is there a higher proportion of bad drivers in Greater Manchester than there are in Northern Scotland?"

 I believe the answer is no - the one or two you might encounter in the Highlands equates to a similar proportion of bad drivers that you encounter in Manchester - it's just that there are far less vehicles on the road in Northern Scotland, so the perception is that driving standards are better there (or any other low population area of the UK).

So that's my take on it. Driving standards are not getting worse, but there are more bad drivers on the road.

Interestingly, despite the continued increase in road traffic in the UK, pedestrian and cyclist accidents have continued to drop over the last 10 years – by approximately 27% and 22% respectively. This is another statistic which seems to buck the trend – surely an increase in road traffic should equal an increase in pedestrian and cyclist accidents, shouldn't it?

Pedestrian accidents have, I believe, reduced due to four main factors - traffic volume, changing social habits, redesigned town centres and paedophiles (bear with me on this one!).

Traffic volume is an obvious one if you think about it - as the volume of traffic increases, the average speed of moving traffic decreases - particularly at peak times when there are more pedestrians on the road - and slower moving traffic is, of course, safer for pedestrians.

People's social habits have changed dramatically in the last 10 years, thanks mostly to the introduction of the Licensing Act 2003. The new act removed traditional licensing hours (11pm for pubs and 2am for clubs) and allowed premises to apply for whatever hours they wanted. If no-one objects under the new act, premises could potentially get 24 hour licences. 24-hour pub licences are actually quite rare, but town centre pubs and clubs now commonly stay open until 4, 5 and 6am.

These later licensing hours have encouraged people to drink at home until much later and then go out much later - it's very common for people to only start arriving in town centres at 11pm, 12pm and even 1am, ready to start their night out.

In road accident terms, this means that drunken pedestrians (along with children, drunks are the most vulnerable pedestrians) are wandering around the roads much later in the night/morning when there are far fewer vehicles on the road. Less vehicles + drunken pedestrians = less pedestrian accidents.

Alongside the changes to licensing hours, more and more town centres have become traffic-free. Pedestrianising town centres has also made the night-time economy areas much safer for drunken pedestrians. In addition, the proliferation of out-of-town shopping centres, and the massive rise of internet shopping has seen people's shopping habits change dramatically, with a further separation between traffic and pedestrians.

On to paedophiles - or to be more accurate, the increase in people's fear of paedophiles. I don't believe there has been a huge increase in the number of sex offenders, but their activity has been publicised much more in recent years and this has resulted in a perception that there has been a huge increase in paedophile activity.

When I was a child, we'd be allowed to play out in the street in the evenings without any fear of being grabbed off the street by Jimmy Saville, and we'd be allowed to walk to school on our own without any thought that Gary Glitter might be hiding behind a hedge.

These days, parent's fears for their children mean that they simply do not let their little darlings walk to school any more, even if it's only a few hundred yards away. It's the same reason parking outside schools has become such an issue in recent years. Rightly or wrongly, parents are far more protective these days and this has dramatically reduced the number of children (and especially primary age children) walking to and from school or playing in the street. When you do see young children walking to school, it's often in the form of a "walking bus" where they're all together, wearing high-viz and accompanied by one or more adults.

So, a number of different social factors seem to me to have had the unintended consequences of reducing pedestrian casualties.

And now it's over to you – if you can start to apply some of the things I've outlined in this book, you can hopefully become better at avoiding accidents – and at avoiding other people's accidents too.

So there you go – that's **How Not to Crash!**

About the Author

Reg Local joined the police in 1990. In 1995 he qualified as a class 1 advanced driver and worked as a traffic officer until 1999 when he qualified as a police advanced driving instructor.

He has taught everyone from learners to experts and has a passion for sharing his knowledge and experience.

He left the police in 2009 and now works in local government.

His first book "Advanced & Performance Driving" was published in 2015 and has been a regular bestseller on the Amazon charts for automotive books.

Lightning Source UK Ltd.
Milton Keynes UK
UKOW05f1838020117
291144UK00008B/223/P